Kind Words and F...

By carefully updating some of Edwards' ...
greatest theologian to point a new generatic...
sinfulness of sin, and the gracious power of ...

Buddy Gray, Pastor of Hu...

Jason has blessed us by opening up the works of Jonathan Edwards with updated style and vocabulary, so that we can benefit from perhaps the greatest intellect ever produced by God's grace in our country and, therefore, contemplate biblically why the Lord our God has made all things, including us, for His glory, which is our joy.

Dr. Harry L. Reeder III, Pastor/Teacher of Briarwood
Presbyterian Church, Author of *From Embers to a Flame*

Jason Dollar has done an excellent job in making available to the church one of the most important of Edwards' works in accessible modern prose. It is my hope and prayer that this book not only introduces readers to Edwards, but more so to the Christ that Edwards sought to exalt. Soli Deo Gloria!

Dr. Steven B. Cowan, Assistant Professor of Philosophy and Religion,
Lincoln Memorial University, Author of *The Love of Wisdom*

Jonathan Edwards is, without question, one of the great minds of the Christian tradition. Unfortunately, Edwards is often lauded but rarely read, because he is such a difficult read, both in the depth of his thoughts and in archaic writing style. Jason does us a great service, making the first more accessible by updating the second. Reading this classic work allows your affections to be stoked by the Spirit!

Dr. Kyle Strobel, Assistant Professor of Spiritual Theology and Formation,
Talbot School of Theology, Biola University, Author of *Formed for the
Glory of God: Learning from the Spiritual Practices of Jonathan Edwards*

Jonathan Edwards has been limited to droll high school history class readings of Sinners in the Hands of an Angry God. We have missed the depths of his masterful exulting in God's glory. What Jason has provided for us, then, is invaluable to the recovery and promotion of perhaps America's greatest philosophical thinker. In this book it is as if Dollar has both polished the diamonds and given us the lenses to better behold them. Read, study, enjoy, and worship Christ through this book.

Jared C. Wilson, Pastor of Middletown Church,
Author of *Gospel Deeps: Reveling in the Excellencies of Jesus*

Also by Jason Dollar

*Contend: A Survey of Christian Apologetics
on a High School Level* (with Bradly Pinkerton)

*Sinners in the Hands of an Angry God:
Updated to Modern English*

*The Excellency of Christ:
Updated to Modern English*

The End for Which God Created the World

Updated to Modern English

The Jonathan Edwards Classic

Updated for Modern Readers by
JASON DOLLAR

The End for Which God Created the World:
Updated to Modern English

Copyright © 2014 by Jason Dollar
Published by Glory Focus (www.gloryfocus.com)

Previously published in
The Reason God Made the World
(Westbow Press, 2013).

All rights reserved. No part of this publication may be reproduced, stored in a retrieval system, or transmitted in any form by any means, electronic, mechanical, photocopy, recording, or otherwise, without the prior written permission of the publisher, except as provided by USA copyright law.

Unless otherwise indicated, Scripture quotations are from The Holy Bible, English Standard Version®, copyright © 2001 by Crossway Bibles, a publishing ministry of Good News Publishers. Used by permission. All rights reserved.

Printed in the United States of America.
Printed by Createspace, an Amazon.com Company

ISBN-13: 978-1505460438
ISBN-10: 1505460433

To
Page, Noah, Anna, Mary, Isaac, and Eden
and to the members of
Rock Mountain Lakes Baptist Church

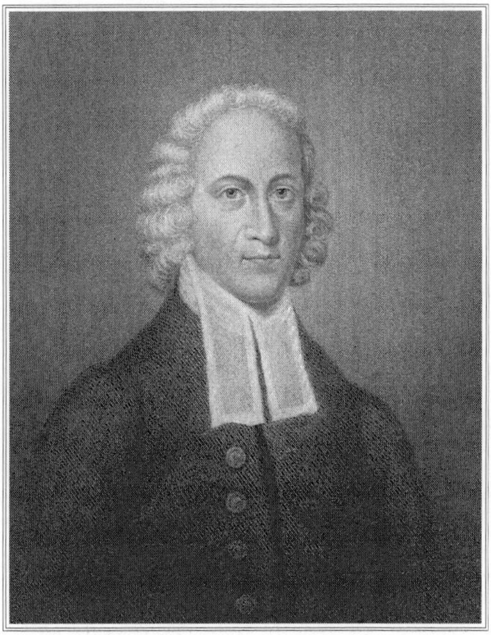

Table of Contents

Introduction..8
1. About Chief Ends and Ultimate Ends..15
2. More about Ends and How They Work......................................20
3. God and Ultimate Ends...24
4. First Division: Help from Reason..30
5. God's Obligation to Be His Own Ultimate End..........................35
6. God's Flowing Glory...46
7. God's Supreme Respect for Himself...54
8. God's Glory in Communicating Himself....................................61
9. The Objection of Inconsistency..66
10. The Objection of Selfishness..75
11. The Objection of Unworthiness..80
12. The Objection of Freeness and Obligation.................................88
13. Second Division: What Scripture Teaches..................................97
14. Scripture on God's Glory as His Ultimate End.........................111
15. Concerning the Moral Part of Creation....................................119
16. Redemption in Jesus for the Glory of God...............................129
17. Judgment Day and All Works of Providence...........................139
18. For the Sake of His Name...145
19. An Arena for His Perfections to Be Known.............................152
20. For the Praise of His Eternal Glory..159
21. The Good of the Creature and the Glory of God.....................164
22. The Happiness of God's People..172
23. Scripture on the Internal Glory of God....................................178
24. Scripture on the Communicated Glory of God.......................184
25. Viewing and Praising God's Glory...194
26. God's Ultimate End Is One...202
27. Conclusion: Eternally Growing Union with God....................209

Outline..217
Acknowledgments..224

Introduction

The written work of Jonathan Edwards is a world of God-focused intensity, biblical depth, joyful worship, logical precision, and personal challenge. My prayerful goal for this book is that God would use it as a tool to propel people into his writings. However, this is only a subordinate goal. The ultimate end I have in mind is to lead people to Edwards because Edwards will inevitably point people to Christ. And when Christ is truly and clearly seen, valued, and praised, then God is glorified. So the glory of God is the ultimate end of this book. It is also the ultimate end of all human life and, indeed, all of creation.

I strongly believe that modern people, Christians and non-Christians alike, need to hear the depth and passion of Edwards anew. These modern English updates are a meager attempt to raise interest in his ministry, especially since his ministry was focused so intently on consciously maximizing the glory of God.

Why Edwards?

There are many great pastors and theologians whose writings seem archaic to modern readers. Why should Jonathan Edwards be singled out among them? Why should his writings be chosen for these updates into modern English?

A major part of the answer has to do with Edwards the man. His pious manner of life, his vibrant relationship with God, his approach to theology, and the highs and lows of his pastoral ministry, were all intriguing to say the least. It is no surprise that many are interested in his life and writings.

Plenty of helpful biographies have been written about Edwards. I certainly commend them to you, especially George Marsden's monumental work, *Jonathan Edwards: A Life* (Yale University Press, 2004). I will certainly not attempt to duplicate those works here. Biography is not my goal.

However, suffice it to say, much of what motivated me to choose Edwards was the man himself. After all, Edwards loved God, not perfectly as he would be the first to admit, but he radiated with holy desire for the Lord. This is clear from the way he wrote, preached, and certainly in the way he ordered his life.

We modern people need examples to show us what love for God looks like. Though Edwards loved God in a much different social context than ours, nevertheless, he offers us a timeless paradigm of devotion to the Lord. Besides, true devotion and love for the Lord has a powerful way of transcending all cultural differences. No matter when or where he lived, Edwards provides a wonderful example of a life spent for the glory of God.

Edwards also loved learning. He was a preeminent scholar with a tremendous understanding of many different disciplines. As a thinker he was interested not only in how things work, but also in how they ultimately connect together. This seems to be why he was a student not only of theology, but also of philosophy, history, and science, among other major areas of thought. As his ideas expressed in this volume indicate, he sought to show how all these things unite together at a common core.

The world today seems saturated with the brokenness and disconnectedness that is often associated with the postmodern worldview. Among many people the hope of discovering a central, unifying concept that holds everything else together seems to have been hopelessly abandoned. This is a tragedy that leads to the perceived loss of meaning and value both in the scope of world history and in individual lives.

In stark contrast, Edwards believed and logically supported the idea that God does all things for his own glory and that this is the ultimate and central reality upon which all other truths hinge. This axiom – God does everything for his own glory – is both biblical and true, and it provides the needed foundation for all authentic thinking and living. The modern world should reflect deeply upon this great axiom and about how it guides and guards our lives. Reading Edwards helps us understand it to some degree and, hopefully, live consistently with it.

So, Edwards was both preacher and scholar, a combination which led to the production of hundreds of deep, powerful sermons and a number of impressive philosophical treatises. In the work featured in this book, *A Dissertation Concerning The End for Which God Created the World*, Edwards reveals his deep understanding of God and the way he has ordered the universe to operate, including the way he has ordered human society to operate. God created the world and all the people in the world for his own glory and for the joy of his redeemed bride. The way Edwards arrives at and supports this great truth is more than enough reason to choose him (and this work in particular) for a modern English update.

WHY ME?

I am not a professional scholar and certainly not an Edwards scholar. Likewise, God has not gifted me to think original or profound thoughts on a high level, as he did with Edwards. But I am a pastor, and part of my calling involves the popularizing of truth. In this present work, I feel that my role is to take Edwards' high thoughts and share them – popularize them, dare I say – with ordinary folks in the modern world.

I am especially interested in those ideas of Edwards' which point people towards the glory of God. Christians need constant reminders of how amazingly glorious our great God really is and what his glory means for our lives. Reading Edwards always provides a refreshing recollection of the absolutely awesome nature of the Lord and what it means for his people that his brilliant glory shines eternally.

However, though I am greatly benefited by reading Edwards, alas, I find him difficult to read. I don't think I am alone in the struggle; many modern readers set aside the writings of Edwards for the same reason. The difficulty does not arise because Edwards was a poor writer, nor because he wrote in such a lofty way that average people can't read him. Rather, it mostly has to do with *when* he was writing. People simply wrote differently in the mid-1700s than they do today. Modern readers typically have a hard time following the decorated prose of writers from Edwards' era.

In fact, this project actually began because I wanted to understand exactly what Edwards was saying in his most famous sermon, *Sinners in the Hands of an Angry God.* The more I read it, however, the more confused I grew. Though I made noble attempts, I could not fully follow the logic of the sermon. So merely as a way of trying to better understand him, I began rewriting the sermon in my own words. I was careful not to change any of Edwards' thoughts but simply update them into modern English.

Once the entire sermon was completely updated, I read through it. I was amazed as I was able to focus on the actual points Edwards was making instead of attempting to unpack and understand the grammar of his lengthy sentences and paragraphs. This, of course, made the sermon much more powerful to my modern English mind.

To demonstrate how helpful a modern English paraphrase can be, here is a brief comparison of a portion of Edwards' original wording from *The End for Which God Created the World,* followed by my updates.

Edwards' Original

> John xii. 27, 28. "Now is my soul troubled, and what shall I say? Father, save me from this hour: but for this cause came I unto this hour, Father, glorify thy name." Christ was now going to Jerusalem, and expected in a few days there to be crucified: and the prospect of his last sufferings, in this near approach, was very terrible to him. Under this distress of mind, he supports himself with a prospect of what would be the consequence of his sufferings, viz. God's glory. Now, it is the end that supports the agent in any difficult work that he undertakes, and above all others, his ultimate and supreme end; for this is above all others valuable in his eyes; and so, sufficient to countervail the difficulty of the means.

Modern English Update

> **John 12:27-28** Now is my soul troubled. And what shall I say? "Father, save me from this hour"? But for this purpose I have come to this hour. Father, glorify your name.

The context of this passage describes Jesus' journey to Jerusalem, where he expected to be crucified within a few days. As he drew near, the prospect of his last sufferings was extremely terrible to him. Under this heavy distress of mind, Jesus provided support for himself by considering what the outcome of his sufferings would bring, namely, great glory to God.

When an acting agent decides to engage in a difficult work, he needs help to succeed in it. If the end of the work is a wonderful end, he can find help by reminding himself of it. When he remembers that the goal, when achieved, will be simply amazing, he finds strength and support to face the difficulties of the work and not to give up.

This short example hopefully shows the goal of readability I have in mind for this update of Edwards' classic treatise. However, I should stress what I hope the example portrays – readability does not come at the expense of losing anything Edwards meant to say. In other words, I hope when you read, you read Edwards, not me.

I should give a fair warning to those encountering Edwards for the first time. Reading *The End for Which God Created the World* can be a challenge even in modern English! However, don't give up on it. If possible, trudge faithfully through it. I can personally attest to the power of this work when the truths of it are firmly grasped. Indeed, rather than the reader grasping the truths, the truths over time begin to grasp the reader!

As an aside, it should be noted that one of the most influential and popular theologians of the past century, John Piper, considers Edwards' essay to be one of the most powerful works ever written outside of the Bible. In his book, *God's Passion for His Glory* (Crossway Books, 1998), Piper writes extensively of the monumental influence Edwards has had on his life and thinking, especially in the great dissertation. My prayer is that Edwards' God-glorifying work will continue to influence the hearts and minds of modern Christians for the sake of Christ, as it has with Dr. Piper.

Perhaps updating the language to modern English can be a tool that helps make that happen.

It is important for me to be clear about something. I don't consider myself to be an authoritative modern interpreter of Edwards. I am absolutely positive that true scholars of this man, who have a deeper and wider understanding of and appreciation for the context of his writings and theology, may not agree with some of the wording I have chosen in this update. Some may not agree that modern English updates should be done at all! For this reason I welcome dialogue. I believe that as a community we can understand Edwards and his theology better than any individual can.

I truly desire to honor Edwards and the God he worshipped so deeply. I hope that nothing at all in this book would give any impression otherwise. If there are mistakes in my interpretation of Edwards, they are my mistakes, not his, or anyone else's.

For this same reason, I want to point readers back to Edwards' original texts. All of his works, including *The End for Which God Created the World* in its entirety, are currently available free of charge online at the Jonathan Edwards Center at Yale University. What he actually said and wrote is much more important and authoritative than my modern English update ever could be.

Why You?

If you are reading these words, then you are a truly connected part of this work. You may be a pastor, theologian, seminary student, or someone who is accustomed to reading theology. Or you may be a lay Christian who loves the Lord but who is not in a vocation that requires the reading of this type of material. You might even be someone who doesn't follow Jesus Christ but who is interested in Edwards for a different reason, perhaps historical or biographical. I believe that whoever you are and for whatever reason you have obtained this book, God has sovereignly designed the flow of your life to put Edwards into your hands.

Therefore, as I write this introduction, I am praying for you, asking God to enable his glory to shine through your study of this work. Dear

Lord, will you use these updated words to either introduce this reader to Jonathan Edwards or expand his or her understanding of Edwards' writings? Will you help the reader clearly see the heart of this man you have used so greatly in the past, and continue to use so wonderfully in the present? Furthermore, Lord, and most importantly, will you use Edwards once again to point people to Christ in order to ultimately glorify yourself for all of eternity? Great sovereign King, your glory is our greatest joy: "For from him and through him and to him are all things. To him be glory forevermore. Amen" (Rom. 11:36).

Jason Dollar
Birmingham, AL
December 11, 2014

Exodus 14:18

The Egyptians shall know that I am the LORD, when I have gotten glory over Pharaoh, his chariots, and his horsemen.

1
ABOUT CHIEF ENDS AND ULTIMATE ENDS

INTRODUCTION

In this work my aim is to answer this question: Why did God created the world? In presenting the answer, I will speak of various types of ends and seek to show what end in particular God had in mind for creating the world. An end is basically a goal, purpose, or reason.

Naturally, seeking to understand the reason God created the world can cause much confusion. To help avoid it, I will introduce our subject by explaining some of the terminology used in the discussion and laying out some general positions about the matter.

I. Explanation of terms and general positions

To begin, a distinction must be made between the *chief end* someone has in mind when they do something and their *ultimate end*. These two phrases do not mean exactly the same thing. Every chief end is also an ultimate end, but it doesn't work the other way around. Not every ultimate end is also a chief end. To help clarify, consider the opposites of the two phrases: A chief end is opposite to an *inferior end,* while an ultimate end is opposite to a *subordinate end*.

A. Understanding subordinate ends

A subordinate end is something an acting agent seeks after only to get at something else more important to him. The subordinate end is not wanted because it is valued on its own account, but is only desired as a means of aiming at some further goal.

For example, suppose a man is inflicted with a disease and goes on a journey to find medicine. Obtaining the medicine is merely his subordinate end. He doesn't want to find medicine for medicine's sake, but rather as a means to a further end, which is healing and restored health. If the medicine couldn't help in obtaining the further end of restored health, then it would be considered worthless, and the man would not desire it at all. Thus the medicine is merely a subordinate end.

B. Understanding ultimate ends

An ultimate end (also called a last end) is something a person seeks after *for its own sake*. He wants it because he loves it, values it, and takes great pleasure in it *simply because of what it is*. He doesn't go after it only as a means of obtaining something else.

When a man loves the taste of a particular fruit, he may work hard and spend a large sum of money to obtain it. The taste of the fruit brings him great pleasure, and since he loves his own pleasure, he values the fruit simply for what it is. He doesn't buy it as an attempt to obtain something else that might bring him pleasure. He wants the fruit for the fruit's sake. In this case the fruit is his ultimate end.

C. Relationships between subordinate and ultimate ends

Some ends are subordinate not only to an ultimate end, but also to other subordinate ends. Indeed, there might be a chain of successive subordinate ends, one dependent upon another, each of them connected in a line until they arrive at the ultimate end. One subordinate end might be sought in order to obtain the next subordinate end, and that one sought for the sake of the next one. This could go on in a long series until the agent obtains what he is really seeking after for its own sake.

For example, a man might sell his garment to obtain money. He then uses the money to buy tools, which he then uses to till his land. The land is tilled in order to grow and obtain a crop, which he then uses to produce food. Finally, the food is eaten and gratifies his appetite, which is what he wanted. The gratification of his appetite is what he was seeking ultimately and what had value in itself for him.

In this illustration the end of selling his garment was to get money, but the getting of money was *only a subordinate end.* It was subordinate not only to the last (ultimate) end, which was gratifying his appetite, but it was also subordinate to the nearer end of buying the tools. However, the tools were only purchased as a means of obtaining something else too, namely, the ability to till the land. But tilling the land was not done for its own sake either, but rather so that a crop could be grown. But the growth of the crop was not an ultimate end either, since it was not sought as an end in itself. It was only sought so that food could be made from it. But producing food was still not the ultimate end, for merely possessing food wasn't valuable to the man as an end in itself. Rather, the food was for the sake of eating and gratifying the appetite. Thus the man's ultimate end was the gratification of his flesh. It was the last link in the chain, where the man's aim and pursuit stopped and rested. He had finally hit his target, obtaining the thing he was aiming for in the entire process.

So when a man comes to find the thing in which his desire terminates and rests, the thing valued on its own account, then he comes to an ultimate end.

Clearly, the chain may be longer or shorter depending on the particular situation. It might be that there is only one link in the chain, only one step he takes, before coming to his ultimate end. This is the case when a man puts honey in his mouth to enjoy the taste of it without aiming at anything further. So in some cases, the end an agent has in view might be both his immediate (next) end and his ultimate (last) end.

To summarize, whatever end is sought for the sake of itself *and nothing further* is an ultimate end. It is the last step in the process, since it is pursued for its innate and intrinsic value. At this ultimate end, the aim of the agent stops, rests, and goes no further, since it has arrived at the good thing which the agent believes to be the reward of his pursuit.

Sometimes a person will seek after something that has the nature of both an ultimate end and a subordinate end. The thing might be sought partly for its own sake, but also partly for the sake of some further end.

For example, a man may seek after the friendship of a particular person partly because it seems really good to be loved and esteemed by others. In this respect he is seeking after the friendship for its own sake, which is an ultimate end. But he may also have another motive in his seeking, to find help with some of the issues he faces in his life – something a true friend could help with. In this respect the friendship is a subordinate end, used as a means to obtain the further end of receiving help with his life. So in this case the man is seeking only one end (friendship) that can be classified as both ultimate and subordinate.

D. Understanding chief ends

A chief end (also call a highest end) is different from an ultimate end. A chief end is not the direct opposite of a subordinate end, but rather of an *inferior end.* The chief end is the most valued end, the one most wanted by the seeking agent.

Some ends will be valued more than other ends. However, just because one end has more value than another doesn't mean it will necessarily be an ultimate end, valued for its own sake. This is evident and will be clear if you consider the following points.

Two ends might both be precious in themselves and both sought after in the same actions, and yet the seeker will value one of these ends more than the other. Plus his seeking will be more serious for the end with higher value.

For example, a man may take a journey seeking enjoyment and pleasure from two different objects. He wants both and values them both for their own sake. But one of them is much more important than the other one, so he sets his heart chiefly upon the more valuable one, seeking after it most of all on his journey.

Perhaps the first thing the man is searching for is a bride to be his beloved wife. Secondly, he longs for the opportunity to look through a powerful new telescope of extraordinary quality, primarily to satisfy his curiosity about it. Both of these are ultimate ends, neither one of them is subordinate to the other or to any other end. But finding his beloved bride would probably be his chief end, while looking through the telescope would be his inferior end. His heart is set vastly more upon his bride, even though both are ultimate ends.

Some subordinate ends might be more highly valued and sought after than some ultimate ends.

For example, another man might be going on a journey seeking after two different things. First, he wants to visit his friends, and second, he intends to receive a great estate or a large sum of money that is waiting for him at his destination. This second aim of receiving the money may be a mere subordinate end. He may not value silver or gold on its own account, but rather the pleasure, gratification, and honor this money can bring him. That is his ultimate end, not the money itself, which is valued only as a means of getting something further. But obtaining the money, though it is only a subordinate end, may actually be more valued than the pleasure of seeing his friends, which is an ultimate end valued for its own sake. If it is, then we have a case of a subordinate end being more highly valued than an ultimate end, thus, being the chief end of the man's journey.

Much more needs to be said about these issues in order to gain a greater understanding of God's reason for creating the world. In the next chapter, we will explore in greater depth these different types of ends and how they work.

2
MORE ABOUT ENDS AND HOW THEY WORK

Having introduced the concepts of subordinate ends, ultimate ends, and chief ends, we now move to expand on these.

II. Expanded explanation of terms and general positions

Under this second introductory heading, nine statements regarding subordinate ends, ultimate ends, and chief ends will be given. These will help us tremendously as we seek an answer to our question: Why did God create the world?

> A. Subordinate ends can never be more valuable than the ultimate end(s) to which they are subordinate.

Towards the end of the previous chapter, it was stated that some subordinate ends can be more valuable than some ultimate ends. However, by saying this we do not mean that a subordinate end can be more valuable than the ultimate end(s) *to which it is subordinate*. After all, a subordinate end has no value at all, except what it derives from its ultimate end. This is precisely why it is called a subordinate end. It is not valued for its own sake. It is sought after and considered precious only because it leads to a further end or because it exists for the sake of the ultimate end.

On the other hand, a subordinate end might be more valued than some other ultimate end to which it is *not* subordinate. In this case the subordinate end is in a different series or chain of ends, and so it is independent of the ultimate end.

The story in the last chapter illustrates this point well. When the man went on his journey to receive his money, it was impossible for him to value the money itself more than the pleasure and honor the money could bring. Having the money was a mere subordinate end, not to be sought for its own sake, but for another end. It would have been absurd for him to value the means more than the end, since money has no value in itself. He wanted the end result that the money could bring.

However, he might have valued the money, which was only a subordinate end, more than some *other* ultimate end to which the money was not subordinate. This other ultimate end was not connected in a series of ends with the money. For example, he may have valued the subordinate end of receiving the money more than the comfort of a friendly visit, which was one of the ultimate ends of his journey.

So a subordinate end is never superior to the ultimate end to which it is subordinate.

B. The ultimate end is always superior in value to any of the subordinate ends connected to it.

In fact, the ultimate end is not only equal, but always more valued by the person seeking it. Keep in mind, the subordinate ends referred to here are in the *same series of ends* with the ultimate end. They are connected to it.

There are some cases when there is an exception to this general rule. In certain circumstances there may actually be equality of value between the two ends. But this only happens when the ultimate end *depends entirely* upon the subordinate end and is understood to be connected to it in a necessary and essential way. In these kinds of cases, no other means of obtaining the last end is possible except through the attaining of the subordinate end. This is why the subordinate end may be valued just as much as the ultimate end. Equality of value comes only because the last end depends so completely and certainly on the subordinate end and can only come into being through it.

For example, consider a pregnant woman who is craving a type of rare fruit that can only be found in her friend's garden. Her friend lives quite a distance away. So the woman sets out on a journey to her friend's house. She is on the journey in order to step into the garden and obtain the fruit she craves. Satisfying her appetite is the ultimate end of her journey. Obtaining the fruit is the subordinate end. But she understands that her appetite will not be satisfied *in any other way* except through the obtaining of the fruit. She is also certain that the fruit will, indeed, work very well in satisfying her craving, if she could obtain it. In this case she values the obtaining of the fruit just as much as she values the gratification of her appetite.

However, if the ultimate end and the subordinate end were not linked together in this way, it is clear that she wouldn't value them the same. Suppose this woman has serious doubts about the ability of the fruit to satisfy her craving. In that case she would not value the fruit itself as much as she values the gratification of her appetite. Or maybe she knows of a different fruit that might also, at least partially, gratify her desire. Perhaps she is in a position to obtain this second fruit much more easily than the first. Perhaps with this second fruit, she would have no trouble obtaining it, whereas, she might run into a journey-ending obstacle with the first fruit. If that happened, her last end of having the pleasure of gratifying her appetite would be frustrated. Or maybe the fruit alone will not satisfy her appetite without something else mixed with it. In this case her value for the ultimate end will be equal to the value of the *several ingredients combined with each other* as many subordinate ends. However, none of those subordinate ends standing alone will be valued equally with the last end.

All of this to say, it rarely happens among people that a subordinate end is valued equally with an ultimate end. This is because obtaining an ultimate end seldom depends on a single, uncompounded step, nor is it usually infallibly connected with that step. Therefore, the last (ultimate) ends people have are most commonly also their highest (chief) ends over any subordinate ends in that particular series.

C. A being has a supreme end if he has only one end in mind for everything he does.

A *supreme end* is a certain kind of ultimate end. It is reserved for someone who has *one and only one thing* in mind as a goal for everything he does. It is called a supreme end because it is the singular end of all other ends as far as this being is concerned. There may be many types of things he does, but every other end he has in mind is subordinate to his singular, supreme end. And as we have already observed, a subordinate end is never more valued than the ultimate end to which it is subordinate, thus the supreme end is the most highly valued of all.

Moreover, all of the subordinate effects, events, and other things that are brought to pass by this acting agent would be extremely varied, but all of them together unite towards obtaining the one last end. They all contribute their share, but not one of them can be valued alone as much as the supreme, ultimate end of all. They are simply means to the greater end. This seems to be how God approaches his works. We will look more fully at this reality later.

D. An ultimate end is one that is loved for its own sake.

As stated earlier, an acting agent regards his last end as the one he loves for its own sake. It is the last end only if it contains within itself the immediate gratification desired by the acting agent. The agent desires it because he loves *it* and not so that he can merely use it to arrive at something else.

Also, the same could be said of avoiding things that are painful or disagreeable. The acting agent avoids those things that directly cause pain or discomfort. In other words, it is agreeable to avoid things that are disagreeable. This fact is evident and makes sense if we keep clear the meaning of the terms.

Next, more clarification will be given to the nature of the ends people have in mind when they do things. We will also begin considering what God might have had in mind as his reason for creating the world.

3
GOD AND ULTIMATE ENDS

In the previous two chapters, I explained and expanded on many of the terms and general positions regarding the nature of ultimate, subordinate, chief, and supreme ends. We now continue this process of clarification, picking up at the fifth point on the list (see the outline at the end of this book to study the entire list together). Now, we will begin to focus more on the ultimate end God might have had in mind for creating the world.

> E. Seeking a singular thing means
> there can be only one ultimate end.

When an agent is seeking only one thing for its own sake, then there can be only one ultimate end. From what has already been established, it seems obvious that if an acting agent is working to bring about multiple ends that he loves for their own sakes, then he has in mind multiple last ends. He considers many things to be agreeable to him, and he delights in these multiple ends on their own account, not just as means to other ends. But again, if this agent is seeking one and only one thing in all that he does (that he loves for its own sake), then he can have only one last end in mind for all his actions and operations. This would be his supreme end.

But here we must make an important distinction. A thing may be valued and loved on its own account in a *simple, absolute way*. That is, it can be desired and agreeable in a universal, original sort of way. In this case the thing is loved antecedent to and independent of all conditions. No other circumstance is responsible for the value the agent has for this particular thing. Or a thing may be valued and loved only *hypothetically* or as a *consequence* of other things happening first.

To grasp the distinction between these two ways of valuing an end, consider a man who loves society in the first sense described above. He loves it originally. It is perhaps built into him to desire and value it. No other events or circumstances are needed in order to spark his desire for society. Because of this he seeks after a family. But then, after he has a family, he begins to value some other things. For example, he begins to value peace, good order, justice and friendship among the members of his family. These things now become agreeable to him, and he now delights in them for their own sake. Since he delights in them for their own sake, these things may be ultimate ends in many of his choices concerning the governing and regulation of his family. But these things were not his *original end* with respect to his family. He was not seeking a family in order to cultivate justice and peace within his family. These desires were not his last end before he had a family, but rather are the consequences of his now having a family. He originally sought the family because of his love for society. Only now that he has a family does he seek, as last ends, that which tends toward the good order and beauty of family life.

In a similar way, it seems to be that God had some particular good thing in mind *originally* which inclined him to create the world. This thing was valued and desired by God in itself, not because of any prior circumstances or conditions. This particular thing motivated God to bring the universe into existence and to create intelligent beings. But after he created the world, and these intelligent creatures came to be and were placed in various situations, God brought about a wise and just regulation of them.

This wise and just governing of creation is also agreeable to God in itself (not simply as means to another end). After all, God loves justice and hates injustice. These are sufficient reasons for God to deal justly with his creatures and to prevent injustice towards them. But we have no reason to think that it was God's love of justice and hatred of injustice that originally motivated him to create the world and bring intelligent beings into existence. He did not create the world originally just so there would be a place where he could bring justice to bear in various circumstances, even though these are certainly a consequence of his having brought the world and people into being. Instead, we must suppose that there is some other (more original) reason God was inclined to create.

It is certainly true that faithfulness is one of God's perfect qualities. Doubtless, he is inclined to fulfill the promises he makes to his creatures. But God's faithfulness could not properly be what moved him to create the world. Nor could his fulfilling promises be his last end in bringing people into being. But *after* he had created the world and brought intelligent creatures into being, God does then bind himself by promise to them. As a result, his being perfect in faithfulness may move him in his providential interactions with them. His exercise of faithfulness and the fulfilling of his promises may even be the ultimate end of many of his good works of providence in the lower, consequential sense of an ultimate end. Faithfulness and truth, after all, are agreeable to God. He delights in them for their own sake.

This means God may do certain works of providence and have particular ultimate ends in mind in doing these works. But these are ultimate only in the lower sense. They are not the single supreme end of creation. Thus we must distinguish between an original, independent ultimate end and a consequential, dependent ultimate end.

Now it is evident that consequential ultimate ends are actually and truly ultimate ends. They possess the nature of an ultimate end, even though they are dependent on some prior circumstance. Their dependence, however, does not change the reality that they are agreeable to the acting agent in and of themselves. The acting agent wants them for what they are, not merely to use them for the purpose of obtaining some further end.

For example, it seems that a righteous being would find justice an agreeable thing in itself. He would love bringing about justice between two parties that concern him *because he delights in justice* and not simply to obtain some further end. Yet we might also suppose that his desire to bring justice to these two parties depends first upon the existence of these parties, as well as the particular circumstance where justice can be administered. Therefore, I make a distinction between an end that is consequential and one that is subordinate.

F. The original ultimate end alone is what motivated God to create the world.

Combining what has been said so far, the original, ultimate end of creation is *alone* what induced God to first create the world. It was this end and only this end that moved him to bring about the occasions for other consequential ends, as explained in the last point.

Furthermore, the more original the end, the more extensive and universal it is. In other words, whatever God had in view as his primary end, which moved him to originally create the world, will have a governing influence over all of his works. We should constantly keep his primary end in mind when we consider everything he does, including our interpretation of his actions toward the people he made. Everything he does, after all, will be for the purpose of eventually arriving at his single supreme end. This leads to the following:

G. God's ultimate end in creating the world must be the same ultimate end he has for all his works.

If we are using the phrase *ultimate end* in this highest, original sense, then this statement must be true: God's ultimate end in creating the world must be the same ultimate end he has in mind for every single work he does. This idea presupposes that God has just one such end, thus, he aims at this end in both his works of creation and providence.

For example, God made creatures. We must suppose God evermore has in mind the reason he made them. Whatever purposes he uses them for, we should believe that he always remembers his ultimate goal for making them.

However, if we refer to *ultimate end* in the lower sense, God may also have in mind things that are ultimate ends (like justice and faithfulness) but not properly his original, ultimate end for creating the world. Some of his works of providence in particular would fall into this category.

H. God's ultimate end in his works of providence in general is the same as his ultimate end for creation.

When it comes to God's works of providence in general, a distinction needs to be made. When something appears to be God's ultimate end in his works of providence in general, this must also be the ultimate end of the work of creation itself.

To explain, consider that God may engage in an action that is an ultimate end in the lower, consequential sense. Certainly, some of his individual works of providence like justice and faithfulness are just this. His end in that case would not be the same as his supreme, ultimate end of the creation of the world. But this can't be true when it comes to his works of providence in general (meaning all his providential works taken together as a set, not just specific, individual works). The ultimate end of God's works of providence in general must be the same as his supreme, ultimate end in creating the world.

It is right to see this connection, because God's works of providence in general are the same as the general use he has for the world he has made. We could even argue from God's general use of the world to the general end for which he designed the world.

So yes, there are some particular works of providence that are inferior ultimate ends (not the supreme last end of creation), and these are intrinsically valuable and agreeable to God in their particular emerging circumstances. Yet this is only in certain cases and in particular circumstances. But if they are last ends because they proceed from the way God has made and uses the world, then they do not depend upon particular cases or circumstances. Rather, it's just the nature of things in general. This is simply the way God designed the universe to operate.

I. There can be only one supreme last end of God's work.

If there is only one thing agreeable to God originally and independent of all future supposed cases, and this is what he sought to obtain by creating the world, then it follows that there can be only one last end of God's work in this highest sense.

On the other hand, to be fair, there may be several ultimate ends of the creation in this highest sense. But if there are several, they must be properly diverse from each other, each one of them being absolutely independent of any future given cases and each one agreeable to the divine being. Furthermore, all of them must actually be obtained by God in his creation of the world.

Having analyzed these nine explanatory statements regarding how to understand the various types of ends and their relationships to one another, we move next to seek what we might learn about these things from reason. Later, we will look directly to the Bible for answers, but for various purposes, we will first consider what we might learn strictly from human rationality.

4
First Division:
Help from Reason

Now that some of the introductory issues have been discussed, we are ready to consider the first of the two major divisions of this work. In this first division, we will look to the realm of reason to see what it shows us about why God made the world. In chapters 4-12 these sections will be unpacked and explained. The second division (chapters 13-27) will focus exclusively on the biblical data, where we will ascertain the overall teaching of the Bible in relation to the reason God made the world.

The first division is broken up into these four sections:

SECTION I: Some general observations from reason about why God created the world

SECTION II: Some further observations from reason about why God created the world

SECTION III: A list of how God shows a supreme and ultimate respect for himself in all his works

SECTION IV: Some objections considered against the reasonable nature of the arguments made

We will now begin considering each of these in turn.

Section I: Some general observations from reason about why God created the world

In this section we ask: What may or may not be God's ultimate end for creating the world? Before we discuss the observations, which will offer many answers to this question, let me say a word about using human reason to help us find answers.

Doubtless, human reason gives us some information on this matter, but this seems to be an issue properly and finally settled only by divine revelation. After all, if we are seeking to determine the aim of the universe we behold around us, we should consult the Architect who built it. We should make it our priority to listen to and rely upon what *he* has told us about its design and astonishing fabric. He knows his own heart better than anyone else, so he knows better than anyone else his own reasons for creating all things and why everything is designed exactly as it is.

Plus, we must face a difficult reality. By their own power, people cannot come to know even the identity of the Author of the universe, much less his purpose in making it.

Sure, people have improved dramatically in the use of their reasoning skills. Look how advanced the fields of science and philosophy are currently. But still, if we do not have a revelation from the Creator of the universe, then we must realize our deficiencies in settling answers about why he made it. The work of his hands is simply too complicated and too wonderful for us to grasp by our own mental power. We need the one who made the universe to speak and inform us regarding his reasons for creating, or else we will never fully understand why he did it.

But it might be objected that we don't need to use God's revelation as our primary, principle means of coming to know why God created the world. It might be said that reason alone is the *best tool* for coming to know this, especially since the giving of God's revelation has actually improved man's ability to reason and think. And now, since their ability to reason has been so improved, all they need to determine God's purpose is their now-improved reasoning skills.

In response to this objection, we would say that, indeed, God's revelation does shine on people like a bright light shining in a dark place. Yes, it does improve man's ability to reason well. However, as amazing as man's thinking faculties are (they are noble and excellent as gifts from God), by themselves they seem almost helpless.

Of course, we should be thankful for how God's revealed Word has helped us reason better. It has proven to be an ongoing, consistent assistance for mankind. God's revelation helps people use their rational faculties in ways much higher and better than they otherwise could have ever attained on their own. But even though this is true, it would be a mistake to rely upon man's reasoning ability alone in order to seek an answer to why God created the world. Even though we use reason in this process, we should not rely *principally* upon it. Rather, we must seek to be guided primarily by God's Word in coming to an answer. This is especially true considering God has addressed this particular issue specifically.

Nevertheless, I am now going to give several dictates about this issue from the realm of reason. After what was just said, you may wonder why this should be done at all. I do this because there are many disputes and arguments about why God made the world. People often argue against what I think the Scriptures clearly teach on this issue, and they base their arguments on what they call the dictates of reason. It seems to me they are using a mere pretended version of reason! So in order to provide an answer to these critics, I will make some observations from the realm of reason. Through this process it will be clear that reason and the Scriptures actually agree perfectly on the reason God made the world.

Here then is my list of observations purely from what seems rational regarding why God would create the world.

A. God is not in any way dependent upon what he has made, nor did he create the world as a result of some personal insufficiency.

Reason teaches us these facts. Both the Scriptures and reason clearly reveal that God is infinite, eternal, unchangeable, and independently glorious and happy. Nothing within the realm of reason implies that God created the world because he was lacking something he wanted or because he was impoverished in some way. He didn't create the world in order to shore up his perfections or to find missing happiness.

Likewise, God needs nothing from the living creatures he has made. They can do nothing to profit him in any way. He can't receive anything from them. He can't be truly hurt by them. Nothing God has made can ever impair his glory or cause him to suffer in any way. I do not need to back this up with various proofs. Every person who calls himself a Christian universally agrees with this.

The idea that God created the world in order to receive something from the creature makes no sense. Not only is it contrary to the nature of God, but it is also inconsistent with the notion of creation. Think about it. The fact that something is created implies it came to be *out of nothing*. Its ongoing existence and everything that belongs to its being came out of nothing. So the creature's existence depends completely on God. Thus, how is it possible for the creature to add something to God? How could it add something more to God than he was before? You see, it is impossible to make the Creator somehow dependent upon the creature.

B. The existence of God precedes any actions he performs, which means his existence cannot be the ultimate goal of any of his actions.

When something is good and valuable in itself, it makes sense that God should value and respect that particular thing whatever it may be. It is worthy of his pursuit, since it is valuable on its own account just for what it is.

Follow this thought carefully: If this thing is *truly* good and valuable, then God should respect it with an *ultimate respect*. He should seek after it in an ultimate kind of way. In other words, it should be the ultimate end of his actions and operations, if it's the kind of thing he can attain using his divine powers.

The final part of the previous statement is highly important, for it might be that there are some things that are very excellent and valuable in themselves but that cannot be attained by God using his divine powers. The reason he can't attain them is because they are necessarily and in every possible way *prior* to God using his divine powers. That is, God could not use his divine powers at all unless these particular things existed first.

So even though these particular things are of infinite value and are, therefore, infinitely valued by God, nonetheless he cannot make them the ultimate end of his divine works. Again, this is because his divine works *depend upon these things*. None of his works can happen without them.

What things are we talking about? God's existence is one thing, and his infinite perfection is another. These are both logically prior to God's ability to act in any way. If God does not exist, he cannot act. Yes, both of these things are infinitely valuable in themselves, thus, God values them both infinitely, but we can't think that God's goal in anything he does is to obtain these two things! After all, he can't do anything at all unless he already possesses these two things! God's existence and perfection are never the *consequence* of any of his works.

This moves us to the following nuanced conclusion: Whatever is absolutely valuable in itself and is also *capable of being sought and obtained by God* is his ultimate end in creating the world. This leads to our third observation.

C. God's ultimate end in creating the world must have the following three attributes: It must be original or prior to the creation of the world, it must be the most valuable thing in itself, and it must be something capable of being attained by his act of creation.

Whatever this thing is which God deems his supreme end in bringing the universe into existence, it must have all three of these attributes. Since this thing is superior to all other things in value, then it is worthy to be called God's highest end in the creation of the world. This is a major conclusion of our thoughts so far. Make sure you understand it well before moving on.

5
God's Obligation to Be His Own Ultimate End

We are observing from the realm of reason things to help us answer our question: Why did God create the world? In the previous chapter, we concluded that God's ultimate end in creating the world must have the following three attributes: (1) It must be original or prior to the creation of the world, (2) it must be the most valuable thing in itself, and (3) it must be something capable of being attained by his act of creation. We now unfold several more truths that stem from this.

> D. If it is possible for God to be his own ultimate end in creating the world, then he is morally obligated to do so.

This seems most reasonable. Why? Because God, as a perfect and holy being, is infinitely valuable and worthy above all other beings or things, and he is most certainly aware of this fact. He is the greatest of all beings. When it comes to worthiness, importance, and excellence, everything else is absolutely nothing when compared to God. He is simply the best there is by an infinite degree.

So, if God values things that are excellent in their nature and their proportions, then he must value himself most of all. His estimation of himself must be infinitely high, since he is an infinitely excellent being in his nature and proportions. To think that God would value something else higher than he values himself would make him guilty of violating his own nature. He is filled with wisdom, holiness, and moral perfection, and he always does the right thing. Therefore, it is impossible for him to value something higher than he values himself.

Cherishing the most honored

Think this point through carefully. At least part of God having a perfectly upright heart involves his cherishing whatever is highest and most honorable. And he should have the highest regard for things that are honorable *as ultimate ends,* not just things that are valued as a means to some other end.

To take this thought further, God's supremely moral heart must move him to show appropriate respect to things that are the proper objects of moral respect. And what are proper objects of moral respect? The best answer to that question is intelligent beings that are capable of moral actions and relationships. But which intelligent, moral being is worthy of the *most* moral respect? The answer is none other than God himself! So because God's morally upright heart demands him to show the greatest respect to the highest intelligent, moral being, then he is obligated to show the highest honor and respect to none other than himself.

In fact, most of the total amount of respect that God shows should be shown to himself, by an infinite margin. Perhaps it is best to say that *all* (at least in effect) of his respect should be given primarily to himself. After all, compared to him, the worthiness of any other being is basically nothing. All the possible respect and honor that can be given belongs to him, the most worthy being. Truly, he deserves the fullest measure of respect that any moral agent or intelligent being is capable of showing. He deserves the whole heart and nothing less.

Therefore, if being morally upright means showing the honor deserved, then the upright heart must show infinitely high honor to God. It is the right thing to do, since he alone truly deserves it. On the other hand, denying God the highest honor would be unfit and morally wrong.

Since this is all true, God must honor himself with the highest honor possible. This is essentially what it means for him to be holy. His heart is so morally perfect that he must properly honor the most morally perfect being in existence, which is himself. He has a moral obligation to respect and honor himself more than any other thing or being.

Supreme honor shown through God's works

Now, let's take this thought even further. If it is right for God to honor himself supremely, then it makes sense that the honor he has for himself will be clearly seen through both his words and *his works*. This is how God reveals himself, through what he says and what he does. As he reveals himself in these ways, it should be clear to an observer that he is honoring himself supremely through these means.

In other words, if God really honors himself supremely in an infinitely satisfying way, then he will certainly act like it. Not only will he be infinitely satisfied in himself directly, but his actions will be infinitely satisfying actions that bring honor to the being he wants honored, namely, himself.

So we can know what God values most by watching the things he chooses to do. He intends for his works to clearly demonstrate who he is. He wants his actions to reflect their Author. His works are bright lights that reveal what kind of being he is. They truly show us his divine and excellent qualities, especially his moral excellence. His works show us the leanings of his heart and reveal to us his desires, and his moral excellence is highlighted as we see these leanings and desires. Thus we should believe that God desires all his works to show supreme respect toward himself. After all, it is within himself that the highest moral excellence is found.

Help from a neutral third party

As we think about why God made the world, perhaps our pursuit for an answer may be easier and clearer if we imagine what a neutral third party might determine about these things: What should God care the most about? What is the most fitting and proper thing for God to honor most? Whatever it is, it will be seen in the way he creates and sustains the entire universe. A neutral, impartial judge would know this, of course.

Now, let's say that this neutral third party happens to be perfect in wisdom and moral standing. Let's also say that he is not the Creator, nor is he one of the creatures. Instead, he is like wisdom itself personified or infinitely wise justice and morality personified. In other words, the third party is indifferent and disinterested. He is the kind of judge that is focused *only* on determining the truth about how things ought to be, without regard to pleasing any particular person.

What would our neutral third party judge about this matter? He would first determine the order of the whole system of existence. He would carefully analyze human beings and differentiate between kings and subjects. He would properly identify the status of both God and the creatures he made. The judge sees the whole system and concludes who should be most honored and what kind of government ought to prevail in this kingdom of existence.

According to his nature, this judge would weigh things in a perfectly fair way. When the judge determines which parts of existence should be most honored, care would be taken to show that the parts that have more innate existence should be honored more than the parts that have less innate existence. This means that someone whose existence is more independent deserves more honor than someone whose existence is dependent upon something else (like having a mother or being created). Likewise, something that has original (or first or prime) existence deserves more honor than something that came about later. Similarly, the greater part of the whole deserves a greater share of respect than those parts that contain a lesser part of the whole, all other things being equal. Furthermore, the most excellent parts of existence would need to be more highly honored than the less excellent parts.

So the amount of respect and honor granted should always be related to the proportions of existence and excellence both compounded together. The greater degree of honor goes to whatever has the highest amount of greatness and goodness combined together.

God and all of creation on the scales of value

Now, suppose the judge was considering only the created intelligent beings, and not the Creator. He would determine that the system of created intelligent beings, *taken as a whole system* and consisting of many millions of individual creatures, was more valuable than any one individual. This makes a great deal of sense. One individual cannot be better than the entire system of which the one individual is part. The whole is worthy of greater honor and respect. Certainly, one individual can be greater and better than another single individual. In that case, the better individual does deserve greater honor and respect than the lesser individual. But no one individual deserves greater honor and respect than the whole system of created, intelligent beings.

Let us further suppose that this neutral judge considers not only the system of created beings, but also the entire system of being in general. That is, the judge is now looking at *everything* that exists. This includes the Creator as well as all the things he has created. Still, every part of this existence must be weighed as to how important it is, how much existence it has, and how excellent it is. Only then can the judge determine how much honor and respect each part deserves.

But how does this neutral judge make his determination? He must use scales. There must be a balance with two sides. The Creator is placed on one side of the scales and all of creation taken together as a whole is placed on the other. The Supreme Being is weighed against everything else put together. What portion of honor and respect should be given to the Creator? What portion should be given to the entire created order? Imagine the scales that weigh such a thing! All of the greatness, power, and excellence of almighty God weighed against the entire scope of creation taken together, including all living creatures as well as non-living things!

If it is determined that the Supreme Being outweighs all the rest of creation in existence and moral excellence, then the difference of weight needs to be determined. Whatever that difference equals is exactly how much greater the share of honor and respect God deserves over the whole of creation taken together.

But how much does all the rest of creation weigh in comparison to God? Truly, even when taken together as a whole, all of creation is like dust in comparison. The neutral judge doesn't even notice this dust as he weighs them against the Creator! They are too small to notice! They are like nothing, virtually weightless, a bit of vapor that quickly dissipates.

How much honor and respect?

Now, the third party arbiter has the duty to make a determination. How much honor and respect should be given to God? The judge observes the scales. Based on the weight of God versus the weight of all other created things taken together, how much should all created intelligent beings honor and value God?

The judge must also determine how much honor and respect should be shown to God in the things *done* in the created universe. What degree of honor should be given to God in all the actions and proceedings in the whole universe of being? What degree of respect does God deserve in the actions of creating, preserving, using, disposing, changing, or destroying?

Do you see where all of this is going? The Creator is infinite. This means he has all possible existence, perfection, and excellence. *This means he must also have all possible honor and respect.* In every way God is first and supreme. His excellent qualities are the supreme beauty and glory, the original good, and the fountain of all good. This, of course, means that he must in every way have the highest regard and honor.

Furthermore, it is fitting that every other being in existence show God the proper honor and respect he is worthy to receive. Remember, he is God over all things. Every other being is properly subordinate to him, depending upon him for their very existence. Thus he is worthy to reign as the supreme head of all existence with an absolute and universal dominion.

So the entire system of existence ought to show proper honor to God in all they do. Indeed, the whole of creation when encompassed together should respect and honor God in a vastly higher way than it respects and honors anything and everything else. Showing honor to creatures should always and universally be subordinate and subject to the honor shown to the Creator.

Let me make a point of clarification. Whenever I speak of this universal system or the sum total of all existence, I mean the honor shown by the sum total or the group as a whole. Of course, this includes the honor shown by each individual creature, but I am focused on the honor shown by the sum total of all intelligent existence. This includes created intelligent beings as well as *uncreated* intelligent beings. But there is only one uncreated intelligent being. Thus it is right and fitting for the uncreated Creator to show proper honor and respect to the worthiest of all objects, just as it is for created beings.

Everything with a view to God

We must conclude that the hypothetical third party arbiter would make a determination based on all the evidence. In seeking to decide what is most fitting and proper, based on the nature of things, in regard to showing honor and the governing of all of existence, this disinterested judge would decide something like this: The whole universe should do all things with the highest regard for God as the supreme and last end of all. Likewise, all things should be done with a view to God.

The whole universe includes all creatures, both those that are animate as well as those that are inanimate. When we say the whole universe should do all things with a "view to God," we are talking about all its actions, events, and proceedings. Really, we mean the entire series of all events.

Perhaps a metaphoric illustration will help make this point clear. Every *wheel* of the universe should turn with a constant, unchanging regard to honor God as the ultimate purpose of existence. Big wheels as well as small wheels should rotate this way. All should rotate as a system in a perfectly uniform way, since they are all rotating toward the exact same goal.

It is almost like the whole system is being animated and directed by one common soul, moving it all towards the same ultimate destination. Indeed, it is very much like the neutral arbiter I have been describing. He is the one that is perfect in all wisdom and moral standing. It is as though he is that common soul of the universe, and he is governing all of its motions toward the goal of honoring God supremely.

God the only Judge

We have been imagining the existence of a hypothetical third party judge who is not the Creator or the creature. But really, this is impossible. There is no such disinterested person who steps into the world of existence, judging what is fit and fair between the existing parties. But even though it is impossible, the case is still the same. The things that the judge hypothetically determined were most fit and proper are, indeed, what is *most fit and proper in reality*.

How do we know this? Think about it. It is certainly right for God to act always in the most fitting way and according to what is most intrinsically valuable in itself. He does this in every action he performs. Furthermore, there is no doubt that God has clear knowledge of what is most valuable and most fit to do. He knows it so clearly that it's almost like perfect morality is a distinct person who directs him.

So it is true that no third being (besides God and the created system) exists as judge. There can't be any such being. But really, there is no need for such a being. After all, God himself has perfect discernment. He is also perfectly moral and infinitely wise. This point has already been made in extremely strong fashion. Thus because of his perfections, he is the judge over all things. It is his responsibility, therefore, to be the supreme arbiter. It is his duty to state all the rules and make clear how things should be. God has the most absolute, holy, perfect, and infinite attributes, which give him a basis upon which to be a true and fair arbiter of things.

But there may be an objection raised to his being the judge. God cannot be neutral and disinterested, states the objector. He is not a third person who is unconcerned personally about the judgment. Rather, he is an interested party, since he is involved as one of the parties.

But this objection is based on the faulty notion that if a person has an interest in a decision that needs to be made, then that person becomes unfit to be the judge in the matter. His interest will blind him and mislead him in the judgment that he needs to make.

Does this fact make God unfit to be the judge and arbiter of the universe of being? Not in any way. Why not? Because God possesses the qualities of *perfect discernment and absolute justice*. If he were blinded because of being an interested party, then he would contradict his own attributes and perfect nature. He cannot and will not do that.

So you see, there must be some supreme judge who determines what is fit and proper to do in the universe. If there was no such supreme judge, then there could be no order and no regularity to existence. Therefore, it is God's responsibility to state clearly what is most fit to do and what actions conform to perfect morality. It is God who owns everything and who is perfectly fit for the office of universal judge. It is as if perfect fitness and perfect morality was a distinct person. Indeed, we can be sure it is a distinct person, and what he wants to happen will certainly happen.

When we consider these things, I think our minds should quickly grasp the notion that God has not and will not forget himself. Why has God created the world? When God answers that question, *he does not slip from his own mind.* His ultimate goal in creating the world is to plainly show a supreme honor and respect to himself. He has clearly stated this to us. Furthermore, he is self-sufficient, unchanging, and absolutely independent of any other being. Therefore, he is morally obligated to show the highest honor to himself, a fact that he is unable to forget.

Whether this is what God has done (or whether this is even possible) must be considered later. Also, later on, we will be looking at various objections against the idea that God created the world in order to show due honor and respect to himself. For now, we will consider more observations from the realm of reason that support these ideas.

E. Whatever God aimed at in the creation of the world (that is good and valuable in itself) must be what God aims at ultimately.

Reason instructs us that God has a purpose for everything he does. He has a purpose for creating the world and bringing every event into being, aiming at some specific end in every work he performs. He does not haphazardly or randomly perform pointless actions.

The end goal he has in mind must be absolute and original as we have already discussed. Further, whatever that end is, it must be his end in an ultimate sense, his supreme goal for creating the world.

God's nature is perfect, so if something is valuable and worthy in itself in a simple and absolute way, then we know God will value that thing simply for what it is. It is agreeable to him. This is the way a being with a perfect nature operates, always and only valuing those things that are truly valuable. And God's judgment and discernment skills are perfect, so he knows perfectly what is truly valuable. If God, in a simple and absolute way, values something just for what it is, then that thing must logically be the ultimate object that he values above all other objects. How can it be any other way? He doesn't value it just to use it as a means to some other end. He doesn't use it in order to obtain anything else at all. To suppose that he values it merely as a means to some further end would be a direct contradiction to what we are saying about his perfect nature and how ends work. He values the thing in an absolute way for the sake of what it is and nothing more.

So it is abundantly clear, if God values a thing in this ultimate way – for what it is in itself – then this thing must be regarded as his ultimate end. This is especially true when we see him actually seeking that very thing in his works. Thus if God creates the world (or any part of the world) seeking this thing that he values, then we can be sure this is his ultimate end for creating the world, generally speaking. Having established this, we proceed to the next step:

> F. When an effect or consequence is caused by the creation of the world (that is simply and absolutely good and valuable in itself) that thing is an ultimate end in God's creating the world.

God created the world for a good purpose. We know this because that is what has happened. The world itself is evidence that God was intending to attain this good thing or that he was aiming at it. In other words, we can rightly infer what God intends to do by what he actually does. After all, reason is clear that he does nothing arbitrarily or without a design.

To state it another way, whatever God aims at in his actions and works is the exact same thing he values so highly. Whatever God intends there to be, he intends it because he values it, seeking after that thing in all of his actions. If an acting agent intends to get something he values through using certain means, then he is seeking after that thing by those means. And by using those particular means, he is making it clear what he values and the identification of his ultimate end. So based on the last point and this one together, *whatever God values ultimately must be what he is aiming at as an ultimate end in creating the world.*

6
God's Flowing Glory

What can reason teach us about why God made the world? In the previous chapter, we focused mainly on what reason teaches us about God's original, initial motivations in creating all things. We discovered that God has a moral obligation to most highly value the most valuable thing in existence, which is himself. Thus God is morally obligated to make himself his own ultimate and chief end in creating the world.

Now, we will springboard from these ideas into a discussion about consequences. After God created the world, many events occurred and many states of being came into reality. How do these events and states of being (which are the aftereffects of his creative work) relate to his ultimate end for creating the world?

Section II: Some further observations from reason about why God created the world

Reason shows us that absolutely good things are a consequence of God's creative acts. From all the conclusions of the last section, we now proceed to the next logical step, a consideration of those things that came about as a consequence of God having created the world. We are looking particularly at the effects of God's creating that are simply and originally valuable in themselves.

Think about this in question form. What things (that are valuable as ends in themselves) came about *as an effect* of God's having created the world? Answering this question will help us see more clearly God's ultimate end.

As I move to explain this, let me be clear that I'm not giving a tedious metaphysical explanation about this matter. I will not address the issues of what a particular thing must have by nature in order to be fit, admirable, valuable, and all the rest. Neither will I explain what it is about the nature of certain things that makes them worthy of being loved and esteemed on their own account. These subjects, I believe, will make sense if you reflect on them with calm and calculated thought. Having made this clarification, we move now to our observations about these matters.

A. The exertion of God's glorious attributes is something that seems fit, proper, and desirable in itself.

God has all kinds of abilities that enable him to do many amazing things. So it certainly seems right that God would *use* these abilities and that he would desire to show them. These abilities include his infinite power, wisdom, righteousness, goodness, and many other attributes.

But what if the world had not been created? Then even though God has these attributes, they would never be put to use! In other words, the power of God is mighty and sufficient to produce major effects, but unless God had created the world, his power would have simply remained dormant forever. His mighty strength would be useless as far as any effect is concerned. Likewise, God's divine wisdom and prudence in dealing with matters would not be in use. Nobody would see it in action because nobody (other than God) would be in existence to observe it. Unless God had first created both people and situations, the wisdom of God in dealing with people and situations would never be known. The same thing is true about God's justice, goodness, and truth.

Of course, God perfectly knows and understands that he has all of these attributes. And he would have this perfect understanding even if he had never exerted any of his attributes or expressed them in any way. On the other hand, if it is excellent to have the ability to (let's say) be completely just, then certainly it is also equally excellent to *actually carry out justice.* If the attribute is excellent in itself, then certainly the operation of the attribute is also excellent. This means God's works of justice are *equally as excellent* as the fact that he possesses the quality of justice as an attribute. Having the ability to act a certain way is only as valuable as actually acting that way.

Doubtless, God considers his personal attributes to be highly valuable. He delights in them. It makes sense then that God also delights in his attributes when they are being exercised and expressed in proper ways. If God delights in his ability to be wise (and he does), then he will also delight whenever he actually acts wisely. He highly esteems both the ability and the action that comes from the ability. Again, God delights in his own justice and righteousness, but he also delights whenever he carries out justice and executes righteous deeds.

B. It also seems fit, proper, and desirable in itself that the glorious perfections of God should be known by other persons besides himself.

Others besides God, who *know* of God's perfections, should also be able *to see* the actual operations and expressions of them. As just stated, the carrying out of his divine attributes is just as valuable as his simply having them as part of his nature. If it is fitting for God's abilities (his power and wisdom and all the rest) to be exercised and expressed by his actions, then it is also fitting that these expressions be seen and not totally hidden. Human reason shows this clearly.

God does not let his abilities lie eternally dormant, but he uses them to bring about certain effects. These effects need to be seen and known. If there was no other person to watch God express his divine abilities, then it would essentially be the same as if he did not express them at all. God would not need to show himself how powerful he is. He already has perfect knowledge of himself and of what these actions would look like if they were expressed.

This leads us to conclude the following: If God's glorious and perfect qualities are desirable and valuable in themselves, then so are the actual expressions of these perfect qualities. Furthermore, if the works and expressions of God's perfect qualities are valuable and desirable in themselves, so also must be the knowledge of these things.

Therefore, when beings discover God's attributes and works, examine them, and come to understand them, then that knowledge is also valuable in itself. This is not a mere negligible value either! *The knowledge* is valuable in an absolute sense! Indeed, the very light of nature informs us that such knowledge is desirable. This leads us to conclude another amazing reality: *It is an infinitely good thing in itself that God causes his glory to be made known to a glorious society of created beings.*

Do you see the logic in this conclusion? First, God's perfect qualities are excellent in themselves. Second, God's works extend from his perfect qualities, and so they are also excellent in themselves. Third, the expression of God's perfect qualities in his works are to be seen and known by other beings who obtain knowledge of these qualities. Finally, this knowledge is excellent in itself as well. So it follows that it is an excellent thing in itself for a society of created beings to know God and his works.

Furthermore, not only does this society glorify God by knowing his perfect nature and works, but this society *ever increases* in its knowledge of these things for all of eternity. There will never be a point at which the individuals in this society cease to grow in their knowledge of God and his works.

The existence of this kind of society (which is an effect of his creation) is something God counts as infinitely worthy. The type of being he is leads him to value it and regard it as highly precious, because it is truly the best and most fitting thing that can exist. Of all possibilities, the existence of this kind of society fits the reality of the situation better than any other possible scenario. Follow this next argument which will help solidify the point being made.

First, existence is more worthy than non-existence. Likewise, untarnished existence is more worthy than the existence of something that has a defect. Second, all created things are worthy to exist, and they have this worth in themselves. Third, this means knowledge and understanding are things that exist and are, therefore, worthy to exist. Fourth, the most excellent kind of knowledge is knowledge of God and his glory. Finally, the knowledge of God is a major part of the created existence. It is, in fact, one of the highest, most real and substantial parts. Indeed, the knowledge of God is one of the furthest things removed from non-existence and defect.

If you think carefully though these premises and the conclusion, you will see how when a group of intelligent beings have obtained knowledge of God, they have obtained something that is infinitely valuable in itself. As such, it is something that God seeks as an ultimate end (not originally, however, but as a consequence of his having already creating the world – remember the distinction between original ultimate ends and consequential ultimate ends discussed earlier).

C. Other beings should love and delight in seeing and knowing the glory of God.

Since it is valuable and desirable for the glory of God to be seen and known, it also seems equally reasonable to say that when it is seen and known, it should also be loved and delighted in. It is fitting for created beings to show the proper response to the infinite dignity of the glory of God. His glory should be valued and praised as worthy. If the knowledge itself is suitable, then the proper *response of the knower* is also suitable. When created beings encounter the glory of God and have an idea in their minds about the true nature of it, they should be moved! Their dispositions, emotions, and desires should be greatly affected by their knowledge of God's glory!

Think about it like this: If God's perfect qualities are excellent and the knowledge of those perfect qualities is excellent, then it is reasonable to conclude that it is also excellent when people *love and cherish* those perfect qualities.

Think about it another way: It is right for God to love and value his own excellent qualities. This being the case, it is also fitting that he would love and value occasions when others also love and value his excellent qualities. This is clear when we listen to the voice of simple reason.

When a certain being greatly values someone else, he will also naturally love to see the one he greatly values *being greatly valued by others*. Furthermore, if a being greatly values himself, it makes sense that he would love to see others greatly valuing him as well.

As it has been said, knowledge of God's perfections and the actions that proceed from them is a thing valuable in itself. So when beings love the glory of God from the heart, this seems to have a greater and even more special kind of value. This is because the disposition and affections of the heart are where moral beauty is best understood and appreciated.

As we take all these thoughts into mind, we are led next to another conclusion from the realm of reason.

D. The full goodness of God should flow forth as streams from an infinite fountain of good.

In God there is an infinite fullness of all possible good. He has the fullness of every perfect attribute. He has as his very nature all excellence and beauty. Thus he is infinitely happy. Furthermore, all of this fullness is capable of overflowing out of and from God. He can, in other words, *communicate his fullness.* He has the capacity to cause the fullness of his glory to emanate from himself outward to others. This being the case, it seems to be agreeable and valuable in itself that *it should flow.* It is right and proper for the infinite fountain of good to pour out into abundant streams!

God is also a fountain of light. Again, it is fitting and proper for the fountain of infinite light to shine forth brightly, spreading out its excellent fullness and lighting up everything everywhere!

Since this pouring, spreading, and lighting is excellent and good, it must be a perfect and excellent thing for the divine Lord to want to pour it out. After all, this overflow of good, at least in some sense, is a multiplication of itself. This is because the overflow of good coming from the fountain is not the same thing as the fountain. So as it overflows it can be understood as an increase of good in some sense. The fullness of good that is in the fountain is excellent in itself and worthy to exist. Likewise, the overflow of the fountain is also excellent in itself and worthy to exist. If the fountain itself is good, then the emanation, communication, repetition, multiplication, and increase of the fountain must also be good.

Thus it is a fitting thing for the infinite fountain of light and knowledge to shine outward in beams of communicated light, knowledge, and understanding. In the same way, it is fitting for the infinite fountain of holiness, moral excellence, and beauty to also flow out in a holiness that is communicated to other beings. The fountain is infinitely full of joy and happiness, so it is fitting for this joy and happiness to flow out in abundant streams like beams from the sun.

From this point of view, it makes sense to say that the knowledge of God's glory possessed by other beings is also a thing that is good and valuable in itself. And not only is the knowledge of God's glory this valuable, but also the *high estimation and love of God's glory*. It is good and valuable in itself when created beings delight in God's glory and find their satisfaction in it. After all, this knowledge and joy in God comes about as an overflow of God himself. His own knowledge, holiness, and joy all shine forth to be known and loved.

Taking everything into account we have observed so far, it appears reasonable to say that *when God created the world, he had in mind as an ultimate end the communication of his own infinite fullness.* He brought things into existence as a way to show forth his own goodness, glory, and holiness. This was his last end. He created an existence where the fullness of his own good, glorious, and abundant perfections would emanate outside of himself, flowing outward from the core of his being. In this world the fullness of God is communicated and diffused or spread out. This is true even though the fullness of God is certainly original in God, since it is a perfection of his nature. In other words, he never lacked the fullness of these glorious attributes. But his *desire to overflow this fullness* was what moved him to create the world.

Here we need to avoid confusion, if possible. It doesn't seem right to me to say that God was moved to create the world because he wanted to communicate himself *to the creature*. Now, we can say that God's desire to diffuse his glory does incline him to communicate himself to the creature *but only after that creature exists*. However, God was moved to create the world in order to overflow and spread his glory throughout it before the creature existed.

To explain, if God was inclined to communicate himself to an object, then this seems to presuppose the existence of that object, at least in idea form. But the thing that excited God and moved him to create the world seems to have been more of a *general* desire to communicate himself. That is, the divine being simply wanted to overflow the fullness of his divinity and spread around the goodness of his glory. It wasn't merely to communicate himself to a particular creature.

As an illustration of my point, think of a tree. In a manner of speaking, a tree has the desire and disposition to spread around its sap (its life) to every part of the tree. The roots and stock of the tree desire to send the sap out to the branches, leaves, and fruit. Of course, the sap can only be distributed to the fruit *once the fruit actually exists.* But the tree has an *original, general* desire to spread the sap throughout *the entire tree.* In other words, the tree does not desire to spread the sap and life merely to the fruit alone. Naturally, the tree does want the sap to get to the fruit eventually, bringing life to the fruit. But spreading the sap to the fruit is not, properly speaking, why the tree wants to spread its sap around. It desires to spread the sap throughout the tree in general, and this includes spreading the sap to the fruit. Similarly, God desires the fullness of his glory to overflow and spread in general, and part of this general spreading is to creatures, including human beings.

Now, in order to fully appreciate and grasp the truths of these previous points, let me make a few summary statements of them. It is right and proper to suppose that God was inclined, as an original property of his nature, to overflow his own infinite fullness. This motivated him to create the world. Thus the overflow itself was what God aimed at as the last end of creation.

7
God's Supreme Respect for Himself

At this point we have concluded Sections I and II regarding what reason teaches about why God made the world. We've seen that God values himself more highly than he values any other beings or even all of creation taken together as a whole. Furthermore, he values the overflow of his glory through his creative acts and other demonstrations of his divine attributes within the world. Likewise, he values the occasions when other beings see and experience the overflow of his glory and when they respond appropriately to it.

In this chapter we will support these conclusions by unfolding a list of ways God shows a supreme and ultimate respect for himself. In particular we will focus on his various works and how they demonstrate his self-respect and self-love.

Section III: A list of how God shows a supreme and ultimate respect for himself in all his works

For the sake of building the argument, we are going to suppose that the points made in the last section are all true. That is, God created the universe as an arena in which his own perfect attributes and glory can overflow. This was his last end in creation. With that as a backdrop, we are now going to look at how the works of God are all done as a means of bringing supreme and ultimate honor to himself.

Let us be clear about our task. In the last section, we observed several things reason demonstrates to be the *consequences* of God creating the world, things which seem to be absolutely valuable in themselves. Because they are valuable in themselves, they are worthy of God making them his last end in his work of creation. Now, we proceed to ask and answer the following question: If God made these things his last end in creation, how is that consistent with his making *himself* his last end? To ask it another way: How does God show ultimate respect and honor to himself *through* his various actions and works? When all is said and done, we will see that in every action God performs he shows ultimate respect and honor for himself.

I will further demonstrate that it is because God infinitely loves, values, and delights in himself that he also naturally loves, values, and delights in the things he does. We can see by the way God values his works that he is truly placing value upon himself and the infinite fullness of good that is in him.

A. God shows supreme respect for himself through the operations and exertions of his perfect attributes.

The first point I mentioned in the previous section was that God holds his own perfect attributes in the highest regard. This being the case, he must also hold the operations and exertions of those attributes with the same high regard. When God does something, he highly honors what he has done, since he highly honors himself. Furthermore, he knows that his divine attributes always function properly (as they should) and that his attributes are sufficient to carry out what he wishes to do.

Remember, the excellence of his divine attributes is related to the *actual use* of those divine attributes. The excellence of wisdom, for example, is found in planning and doing things wisely. Since God loves himself and his own attributes, he will delight when his attributes are put to use. He will find joy in expressing and exercising them properly.

If a person has a good and virtuous friend who is wise, loves justice, and things like this, then he will delight and praise his friend when he sees him being wise and just. The person will love to not only know that his friend possesses these excellent qualities, but he will also love to see these qualities *in action,* actually working in the world. It is the same with God. He delights and highly values his own perfections and virtues. So we logically expect him to equally value the actual working and expressions of his perfections and virtues. We would also expect him to highly value all the types of effects they cause when they are put into practice.

Now, here is my point: Since God delights in the expressions of his perfections, he is demonstrating that he delights in the perfections themselves. But really, what are these perfections in which he delights? They are simply *who he is;* they are what forms his character. His perfect qualities make him God. So when God delights in his own perfections, he is actually delighting in himself! Thus when he performs any kind of action or work, he does it with the aim and goal of making himself his own ultimate end.

B. God shows supreme respect for himself by loving when others know him, delight in him, and love him.

This clear connection (between God's works and his making himself his own ultimate end) is also seen with the second and third points I made in the previous section. The second point had to do with the desire to have other beings highly prize and delight in a person's excellent attributes.

If a person loves some other person and rejoices in that person's qualities, then he will also consider it excellent when that other person's excellent qualities are known, acknowledged, esteemed, and highly prized by others. Anybody who loves someone or something also greatly approves when others love that same person or thing.

Likewise, he will not approve if others show contempt for that person or thing. This is simply what happens when a person loves another person and places a high premium on the good qualities of his friend. And this is the way it ought to be, so long as the beloved friend is *qualified* to be loved and prized in this way.

What is true of friends is also true of a single being that loves himself highly and holds his own excellent qualities in very high regard. It is right for him to do this, if he is truly the kind of being who deserves to be honored in this way. That is, it is fit for him to love himself and delight in his own excellent and valuable qualities being acknowledged, appreciated, and delighted in. This is proven by the reality that God loves himself and his own perfections. In seeking to have his perfect attributes seen and appreciated as his end goal, God is ultimately seeking and making himself his end goal.

C. God shows supreme respect for himself when his full goodness flows forth like an infinite fountain.

Now, let's think about this in connection with the fourth point made in the previous section. There, we discussed that God has an inclination to communicate abundantly the infinite fullness which he possesses within himself. It springs gloriously from him in all that he does. We are referring to the overflow of his knowledge, excellent qualities, and happiness.

When we think properly and deeply about this, we will see that in overflowing this way, God is making himself his own last end. He is demonstrating very plainly that he has a supreme and ultimate regard for his own being.

It would not be proper to say that since God created other beings and spreads his glory and fullness across creation, therefore, these other beings must be his end. After all, he had the inclination to emanate his glory *before* he made these creatures. Sure, the spreading of his glory is properly considered the thing that gave rise to his creation, including giving existence to other beings. It was the inciting cause of it. However, God had himself as his own end, not his created beings.

Think about it. God's great desire to emanate his glory had to be within him, even in intention and foresight, before the existence of the other beings he made. This is because God's desire to emanate his glory is the foundation upon which his desire to create the creatures is built. He must first have had the desire to spread his glory before he had the desire to create the creatures, or even intend to create the creatures, or even foresee that he would create the creatures.

If that previous statement is true, then how should we understand God's love and care for the creature? It can be taken in either a broad sense or a narrow sense. In the broad sense, it might simply be the good inclination in his nature to communicate and demonstrate the fullness of his being in general. He wants to show his knowledge, holiness, and happiness. Thus he creates people so they can experience these wonderful things.

This broad desire to show the fullness of his being might be called love or benevolence. After all, it flows from the same good nature that is at work in love. Indeed, it flows from the exact fountain where love proceeds, properly and originally speaking. It can be called love also because it has the same general tendency to bring well-being and benefit about in the lives of the creatures.

But his desire cannot have any particular present or future created being as its objective end. Why? Because his desire existed prior to the existence of any such object. And because his desire is the source upon which future objects depend in order to have being at all. And because his desire is not any different from God's love for himself, as we will see more clearly later.

In addition, we can understand God's love for his created beings in a more narrow sense. In the most strict and proper sense, love presupposes the existence of the object being loved. This is true at least in idea and expectation. It might be presented to the mind as something in the future, but it is there nonetheless.

God did not love the angels in this strict sense. Rather, he loved them as a *consequence of his intending to create them.* When he intended to make them, he then had an idea of their future existence in his mind. This means his love for the angels was not what originally gave rise to his intention to create them. Remember, in this strict narrow sense, love presupposes the existence of the thing being loved. The same is true of pity, which presupposes the existence of a miserable suffering object.

So if God does not spread his glory abroad creation ultimately because of love for the creature, then why does he do it? It may be that he is inclined to spread his glory in this way because he desires his glory existing in emanation. God has such deep respect for himself and such infinite desire for and delight in his own glory. This respect, desire, and delight strongly inclines him to assure that his glory is abundantly spread. He is also deeply committed to enjoying the emanation of it.

For an illustration, think once more of a tree. By nature it grows buds, shoots out its branches, and produces leaves and fruit. This natural outworking is an inclination that terminates in its own complete self.

For another illustration, think of the sun. It has such a tendency to shine! It diffuses its full brightness and abundantly spreads its warmth. This shining, spreading inclination of the sun is merely its natural tendency towards its most glorious and complete state.

It seems that God sees himself in a similar way. He must communicate himself! He must emanate his infinite glory and good. These belong to the fullness of who he is, and without these things he would not be in his most glorious or complete state.

Therefore, the church of Christ is called the fullness of Christ. God directs the emanations of glory and the communications of his fullness towards and in the church. It is as though he were not in his complete state without her, just as Adam was in a defective (so to speak) state without Eve. In addition, the church is called the glory of Christ, just as the woman is the glory of the man (see 1 Corinthians 11:7). God says, "I will put salvation in Zion, for Israel my glory" (Isaiah 46:13).

Indeed, *after* God intended to create other beings, we may conceive of him being moved with love and care for these creatures. Then it could be said that he loved them in the strict, narrow sense. He demonstrates this love in the way he deals with them and in the works he does around them. Furthermore, the way he does good things for them and to them might be understood as the source of all of his proceedings throughout the entire universe. His particular focus on these beings is the way he satisfies his own desire to show benevolence. And this desire to show benevolence to them may also be understood as the way God satisfies his general inclination to emanate and spread his own glory.

This means that God's acting for his own glory in making himself his own last end and God's acting for the benefit of the creature *are not to be set in opposition to one another.* They are not mutually exclusive or contradictory. Instead, we should understand them as coinciding with one another. We should also see each one implying the other in itself.

This being the case, we must also understand that God is considered first and original in this regard. The creature is the object of God's regard only by way of consequence and implication. God is the eternal original, and the creation is comprehended, as it were, in God.

So far in our study of how God demonstrates a supreme respect for himself in all his works, we have seen that God infinitely values and delights in the emanations of his full glory in his work of creation. He has the same delight in the infinite fullness of good within him. Thus he has supreme respect and love for himself. Furthermore, when God makes these emanations of himself his ultimate end, he is essentially making himself his ultimate end.

This last statement will become more clear as we consider the nature of God's communications of his fullness and what sort of circumstances surround these communications.

8
God's Glory in Communicating Himself

In the previous chapter, we discussed the reality that in all of his works God is ultimately glorifying himself. In all that he does, he is ultimately showing a supreme respect for his own being. When he exerts his glorious attributes in their proper operations, ultimately he is exalting and honoring himself. He delights when other beings see and know his glory. He further brings glory to himself by graciously overflowing the full goodness of his being into the lives of others.

It is this last point that I intend to expound further. Here, we will especially focus on the specific things God communicates to the creature through his overflowing glory, namely, knowledge, holiness, and happiness. It will be shown that in communicating these things to his creatures, God is ultimately respecting and honoring himself above all.

Glory to God when he communicates his knowledge to the creature

One part of God's divine fullness which he communicates is his divine knowledge. Included in this is the knowledge that his creatures have *of him*. This knowledge must certainly be relevant to God's ultimate end in creating the world, because knowledge of God is the ultimate end of all other knowledge!

All knowledge moves along a continuum towards the perfect knowledge of God. In fact, without the knowledge of God which he communicates to them, creatures would have a broken and vain faculty of understanding. Furthermore, the knowledge that people have of God is most properly understood as a communication of God's infinite knowledge. After all, his infinite knowledge consists primarily of knowledge of himself. Therefore, when God makes the communication of his infinite knowledge to the creature his ultimate end, he is simply making himself his ultimate end. Indeed, the knowledge that the creatures have is nothing but conformity to God. Their knowledge is a reflection of and a participation in God's own self-knowledge. Really, it is the same thing in as much as it is possible for it to be (it is actually an infinite amount less, just as the sun communicates its light and glory only partially through its particular beams).

Besides this, we must remember exactly what it is that God is knowing. The object of his knowledge is his own perfections or glory. Thus in knowing himself, God is glorified, since his own excellent nature is being seen.

So as God values himself and delights in his own knowledge, he must also delight in everything that is part of that knowledge and everything that goes along with it. As God delights in his own light, he must also delight in every beam of that light. As God places high value on his own excellent nature, he must also be pleased when that excellent nature is made known and glorified.

Glory to God when he communicates his holiness to the creature

Another area where we see the emanating overflow of God's divine fullness is in the communication of virtue and holiness to the creature. The creature can receive this communication and experience God's moral excellence, which is, properly speaking, the beauty of his divine nature. Now, just as his own beauty brings God great delight, he must also delight in the holiness of his creatures. This is not an option for God, but a necessary reality. After all, their holiness conforms to his and participates in it.

When a jewel is held up to the sun's beams, it shines brightly because the sun itself provides the source for its brilliance. In some way it also participates in the emanation of the sunshine, though certainly in much less degree. This is what happens when God's creatures shine in holiness!

Though much smaller in measure, they find the source of their holiness in God and participate in the shining beauty of his holiness.

But what makes up holiness in the creature? What is the mark in a person's life that he or she is growing in it? Love, of course, since it is the full scope and summary of all true virtue. This love finds its expression primarily in love for God. The person who has this kind of love for God will think very highly of him and spend time contemplating, admiring, and praising his divine attributes, finding rest in them.

But what are these actions that were just listed? They are nothing more than a person's heart exalting, magnifying, and glorifying God the person. As I made clear earlier, this is exactly what God necessarily desires and approves, because he loves himself infinitely and places such high value on every glorious aspect of his own nature.

Glory to God when he communicates his happiness to the creature

In addition to God's knowledge and holiness, he also communicates the fullness of his divine happiness. God's happiness consists in his enjoyment of and rejoicing in himself. And God's joy with himself is exactly what makes the creature truly happy as well.

As with knowledge and holiness, this kind of happiness is a participation in the very happiness of God. Furthermore, God (and his glory) is the objective ground of this happiness. So when God's creatures rejoice in him, finding their happiness in his being, then he is magnified and exalted. Thus joy – which can be defined as the exulting of the heart in God's glory – is one of the major components of real praise.

The end result is as follows: God is all in all in every part of what he communicates of his divine fullness to the creatures he has made. The entirety of the communication is ultimately from him, to him, and for him. After all, what is being communicated *is divine,* something of God's very being.

Also, everything God communicates is the kind of thing that, when received, causes the creature to be conformed and united to God. This conformity and unity to God happens in proportion to the particular type and scope of communication God gives. When the communication is greater, there is more conformity and unity. Furthermore, in the very nature of the communication itself is where the honor, exaltation, and praise of God is found.

Think further about this. The thing God aimed at in creating the world was the communication of himself, which he intended to do throughout all eternity. This is the ultimate end he had in mind. When we think carefully and deeply about the nature and circumstances of God's eternal emanation of divine good, we see the following reality clearly: God, in making the communication of himself his ultimate end, makes himself his ultimate end, showing the highest respect for himself.

Now, we will build on this argument by showing that God not only communicates his fullness to his creature, but he does so in a way that is ever increasing throughout all of eternity. We have many reasons to think that he does this for the purpose of increasing the amount and quality of knowledge the creatures have of him, as well as increasing their love for him and their joy in him.

Also, consider the reality that the more God's divine communications increase to one of his creatures, the more that person becomes unified with God. This is because he is connected more deeply to God in love, and the union becomes more and more firm and close over time. As the communication of glory flows and increases, the heart of the man draws progressively nearer to the very heart of God. Simultaneously, the creature progressively conforms to the image of God, which becomes increasingly more perfect and identifies increasingly more with all that is in God.

In God's eyes this must be an infinitely close nearness. Think of it, God has a comprehensive view of all eternity. He sees this ever increasing union between himself and his creature all at once. He sees the creature's conformity to his image as it is from the eternal point of view. Thus from his eternal perspective, the union and conformity must be a perfect nearness, conformity, and oneness. For it will forever move nearer and nearer to that absolute perfection of union that exists between God the Father and God the Son. Yes, God sees it all perfectly, the full infinite progress and increase. In his eyes, it must be the fulfillment of Christ's request in the following passage:

> **John 17:21; 23** That they may all be one, just as you, Father, are in me, and I in you, that they also may be in us. . . I in them and you in me, that they may become perfectly one.

The chosen ones of God, who have eternity future as the duration of their lives, must be viewed as being, as it were, one with God. This is because they are the end of all the rest of creation and are, in the eternal perspective, made God's ultimate end.

God has shown great respect to these chosen ones. He brought them home, uniting them to himself. He centered them perfectly in himself, and they are, in a manner of speaking, swallowed up in him. Thus his respect for them eventually coincides with (becomes one and the same with) the respect he has for himself. This means the interest of the creature is the interest of God himself. This is true, of course, in proportion to their degree of relation and union with God.

To illustrate this point, consider a man with a family. His interest for himself is seen as the same as his interest for his family. This is because of the close relationship they have with him. He respects and loves them and has a strict and near union with them. But think about God's chosen ones! They have eternity future as the duration of their lives. This being true, they are more near and dear to God than the man's family ever could be to him.

All that has been said here shows that all things are from God as their first cause and fountain. So all things tend towards him and progressively draw nearer and nearer to him for all of eternity. This argues that God, who is their first cause, is also their last end.

9
THE OBJECTION OF INCONSISTENCY

It goes without saying that the conclusions reached so far under the first three sections are not universally accepted by all people. Many objections have been raised. It seems wise to deal with these objections and show how each one fails.

Section IV: Some objections considered against the reasonable nature of the arguments made

Just to be clear, the arguments made so far can be summarized in a brief statement: God made himself his own ultimate end in creating the world. All of the objections we will consider and critique are presented against this particular conclusion.

> *Objection 1:* God seeking himself would be inconsistent with his own character.

Some people might say that what I have deduced is inconsistent with God being an absolutely independent and immutable being. This objection might be raised in particular against the idea that God is inclined to communicate his fullness and emanate his glory *as his most glorious and complete state.* The objector might believe that this idea is not consistent with God being self-existent from all eternity. He is absolutely perfect in himself and is infinitely and independently good. It doesn't seem to make sense to the objector, then, that God aims at himself as his end in the creation of the world. This would seem to imply that God is aiming at his own interests or happiness, which cannot be easily reconciled with God already being perfectly and infinitely happy in himself.

The objector continues, stating that if it were possible that God needed anything, then it might make sense that God would make himself and his own interests his highest and last end in creating the world. But, alas, God doesn't need anything.

Furthermore, if it were possible that the goodness of the creatures God has made might be able to extend to him (or that in some way they could be profitable to him), then there would be some reason and grounding for the conclusions that have been drawn so far. But this is simply not who God is, they say. He is above all need and could have no reason to add anything to himself or advance himself in any way. He cannot be made better or happier in any way, shape, or form.

This being true, what purpose would God have in making himself his own end? Why would he be interested in seeking to advance himself in any way by his works? Can you see how absurd it is to suppose such a thing? Why would God do such great things in order to obtain what he already possesses in a perfect way?

Additionally, the objector could say that from all eternity God has been in perfect and complete possession of all his holiness, perfections, and happiness. He has never needed to add to these things and does not need to add to them now. How then can we conceive of a reason that God would want to seek these things?

Answer 1: Wrong notions of God's happiness

This objection arises partly because many people have come to believe wrong notions about God's happiness. These wrong notions flow from a clouded attempt to understand God's absolute self-sufficiency, independence, and immutability.

Indeed, it is true that God's glory and happiness are exclusively in and of himself. He is infinite, and thus nothing can be added to him. He is unchangeable in his whole being as well as in every part of his being. Yes, he is completely independent of all that he has made, and he does not depend upon the creature in any way.

However, it does not follow from this that God is void of any real and proper delight in the things he does with respect to the creatures he has made. It does not follow that God takes no pleasure in the communications he extends to them. It does not follow from God's perfect nature that he finds no happiness in the effects he produces in his creatures or in what he sees in their qualifications, dispositions, actions, and states. None of these conclusions are true. Rather, God may have real and proper happiness in seeing his creatures in a happy state. It could be truly pleasurable for him to observe their true pleasure.

But his happiness about their happiness may not be fundamentally different from the delight he has in himself, being a delight in his own infinite goodness. God's delight in the delight of his creatures may simply be the exercise of his glorious propensity to spread out his glory and communicate himself. When this is done, it satisfies the inclinations of his own heart.

We must be sure to clarify the point. The delight God experiences in the happiness of his creatures cannot properly be said to be a delight that he receives *from them*. After all, their happiness is only the effect of his work *in them*. Their delight and joy comes as God communicates himself to them, not the other way around. God allows his creatures admittance to participate in his fullness. That is where their pleasure, delight, and joy are derived.

The illustration of the sun and the jewel helps us understand this point. As the sun shines through the jewel, it is the jewel that receives its light. The sun does not receive any light from the jewel. The jewel only shines as it participates in the brightness of the sun.

When it comes to people being holy creatures, God could certainly have a proper joy and delight in this that is consistent with his independence and self-sufficiency. He is the one, after all, who imparts this holiness to them, and again, this gratifies his inclination to communicate his own excellent fullness.

Certainly, God can experience delight as he beholds the beauty of holiness in them, which is an image of his own beauty. His must be a true and great pleasure as he observes an expression and manifestation of his own loveliness, which he has communicated to his creatures. In so doing, it is clear and evident that his happiness is actually in himself. He delights and finds pleasure in his own beauty as he delights and finds pleasure in the expression and reflected image of his beauty.

Look at it from the other point of view. If God *did not* find pleasure in the expression and image of his own beauty, it would be evidence that he did not delight in his own innate beauty. If God did not delight in the emanations and reflections of his holiness, it would mean that God had no happiness and joy in his own perfection. Thus we are to understand that God has real pleasure and real happiness in the holy love and praise of his saints. This is because their love and praise is the result of his communicating his holiness to them, which is then reflected back to him.

If we really understand this, then we should also understand that his pleasure and happiness in his saints and their holiness is not distinct from the pleasure and happiness that he has in himself. Rather, it is a true instance of it. Furthermore, God's delight in the expression of his perfections does not detract from his being glorified in those expressions.

Think about it. God's glory consists in his perfect qualities and in the exercise and expression of them and in the effects caused by their use. For example, God is wise by nature, thus he makes infinitely wise plans. God is also powerful, so he carries out great and mighty deeds. He is also just, leading him to act righteously in what he does. He is also good, which can be seen in how he communicates happiness.

In all these things, both in his nature and in his actions, God is glorified. He is honored and praised as he exhibits and communicates his nature through his actions. He is also honored and praised as people come to know of his perfections and the outworking of them.

Of course, as they come to know these things, people highly praise God himself as a result. When God delights in all this, it does not mean that he is delighting in something other than himself or something other than his own glory. To the contrary, when God delights in the emanation and brilliant shining of his glory, it is a necessary consequence of his delighting in himself and the glory of his own nature.

Additionally, nothing I have said argues at all that God has any dependence upon the creatures he has made in order to be happy. Again, though he experiences true pleasure in the holiness and happiness of the people he has made, his pleasure cannot properly be said to be something he receives from them. Rather, these are the things that he gives to them. They are entirely from him without exception. Therefore, nothing is given to God in the sense that something is added to him. We must understand these things properly. God's rejoicing in his creatures is fundamentally a rejoicing in his own acts and in his own glory expressed through those acts. His joy is not derived from the creature. It is dependent upon nothing else except his own actions, which are exerted with an absolute and independent power.

Yet it is true that, in some sense, God has more delight and pleasure as a result of the holiness and happiness of his creatures. This is because God would be less happy if he were less good. And he would be less happy if he did not have that perfection of his nature that deeply desires to spread abroad his own fullness and glory. His inclination to spread his glory is part of his perfect nature, so if he did not have the inclination, he would be less happy. Furthermore, he would be less happy if it were somehow possible for his good actions to be hindered or for his other perfections and their active outworking to be thwarted.

God has complete happiness precisely because he has all these perfections and cannot be hindered in exercising them as he sees fit. No person or thing can stop him from displaying his glorious works and presenting the inevitable results of such a display. And surely this is not because he is a dependent being! No, it is because *he is independent* that he can't be hindered in his works.

With all this in mind, it appears clear that none of the conclusions in this work are inconsistent with what the Scriptures say about God's nature, not in the least. For example, no conclusion made is inconsistent with the teaching of Scripture that God cannot be profited by the works of man. Nor is any conclusion inconsistent with the scriptural teaching that God receives nothing from us, either by our wisdom or our righteousness. Rather, all of the passages of Scripture that express these realities plainly mean no more than that God is absolutely independent of us. They teach that we have nothing in our own power. We have no resources of our own to give to God, and further, no part of his happiness is derived from man.

None of the conclusions I have drawn so far contradict these biblical truths in the least. Rather, it has been stated that the pleasure God has in the things mentioned is a pleasure in his spreading and communicating himself, his holiness, his happiness, and his glory *to the creature.* Nothing I have concluded would indicate that God in any way finds his pleasure from what he receives *from the creature.* Surely no argument can be made that God is impoverished and needy because he has an inclination to communicate his infinite fullness! Neither is there an argument that a fountain is empty and deficient because it is inclined to overflow! These notions are both absurd.

Back to the scriptural expressions mentioned before. Another thing these expressions signify is that God's happiness cannot be added to or altered by anything that comes from the creature. Simply put, God's created beings are unable to change him, increase him, or decrease him in any way.

None of the conclusions drawn so far infer something other than what the Bible teaches about this matter, not in the least. God's making himself his own last end is in no way inconsistent with his eternality or the absolute unchanging nature of his pleasure and happiness. This is because God's joy in communicating himself is without beginning or change. These communications and expressions were always equally present in his divine mind. Yes, he carries out the communications of himself in time, but his own knowledge of them is timeless. Yes, indeed, the exercises, operations, effects, and expressions of God's glorious perfections – the very things he rejoices in – are taking place within time as we know it. But he *beholds them all* simultaneously, with equal clearness, certainty, and fullness in every respect. He sees them all at the same time, even now. God enjoys them all without variableness or succession as he beholds them perfectly in his own independent and immutable power and will.

So from God's point of view, the joy he experiences in the operations of his perfections in time is eternal, absolutely perfect, unchanging, and independent. Neither his view nor his joy can be added to or diminished by the power or will of any creature. Furthermore, his eternal view and his infinite joy are both fully independent of anything mutable or contingent.

Answer 2: No better alternative

Some may not be satisfied with the preceding answer. These people may continue to insist that the objection is valid, that the idea of God having himself and his own glory as his ultimate end in creating the world is inconsistent with his perfect and unchanging nature.

I would challenge those who are not happy with the answer given above to come up with a better alternative. Can they devise a scheme that isn't just as subject to the full force of this objection, if there is any force in it at all?

Think about it. If God had any ultimate end at all as his aim in creating the world, then there was *some* future thing he was aiming at. What is this thing? In creating the world, he designed things so that his last end would actually come to be. Whatever this last end is, it is agreeable to God and the inclination of his will. This end might be his own glory or, for the sake of argument, the happiness of his creatures or maybe some other end.

Now, if God is seeking this last end that is agreeable to him, that satisfies his desire, then he is certainly gratified when he accomplishes it. It seems obvious that this last end would be something he finds truly desirous, for it is the object of his will. Thus as something he finds truly desirous, his last end is the thing he takes a *real* delight and pleasure in.

But according to the objection, this can't be. How can God have anything future that he desires or seeks after if he is already perfectly, eternally, and immutably satisfied in himself? In that case what remains for God to delight in or be further gratified by? There would be nothing at all, since God's eternal and unchangeable delight is in himself as his own complete object of enjoyment. Thus the objector is caught by his own objection.

Therefore, we should carefully understand that whatever God's last end is, he must have a real and proper pleasure in it. After all, he finds gratification in whatever is the object of his will. This is because whatever he wills after is satisfying to him in itself. Or it gratifies him because it would allow him to obtain something else that would be satisfying to him. But God's last end is what he wills after *for its own sake,* as being satisfying to him in itself. It is the thing he delights in truly. It is the thing in which he finds some degree of genuine and proper pleasure.

In order to say otherwise, we would have to deny that God has a will at all with respect to anything brought about to pass in time! We would have to deny his work of creation! We would have to deny that any of his works of providence are truly voluntary! But we have many reasons to believe that God's works in creating and governing the world are the fruits of his will and understanding.

Furthermore, surely we mean something real when we refer to the *acts of God's will.* Thus if he has a will that indeed acts, then he is certainly not apathetic or indifferent about whether his will is fulfilled. In other words, it certainly matters to God whether his will achieves its purpose, and when it does, he is pleased and finds great pleasure in it.

Taking this thought one step further, if God has real pleasure in attaining the purposes of his will, then when he does attain what he wills, it makes him happy. Whatever God finds any measure of delight or pleasure in, he also finds some measure of happiness in that same thing. To suppose that God only has a figurative or metaphoric pleasure in the things that are brought about to pass in time is an error. It would require one to also suppose that God exercises his will about these things and makes them his end in only a figurative or metaphoric sense.

Answer 3: God's self-sufficiency actually diminished by the opposite view

Upon deeper examination, the teaching that God makes his creatures (rather than himself) his original ultimate end is actually the doctrine *farthest* from shining a favorable light on God's absolute self-sufficiency and independence. This teaching agrees less with God's independence than the doctrine it objects against, namely, that God seeks himself as his own last end.

To clarify, we must conceive of God's workings as depending upon his ultimate end. He depends on his ultimate end in his desires, aims, actions, and pursuits. So God would fail at all his desires, actions, and pursuits if he fails to achieve his end. But if God is his own last end, then he depends on nothing but himself when he depends upon his last end. If everything that exists is of God and to God (if he is the first and the last), then God's dependence upon himself as his last end demonstrates that he is all in all, or he is all to himself. He does not go outside of himself in what he seeks. All his desires and pursuits originate from and terminate in him. Thus he is dependent on none but himself, whether in the beginning or in the ending of any of his actions and operations.

On the contrary, suppose God makes the creature his last end rather than himself. In this scenario, since he depends upon his last end, God would in some way be dependent on the creature. But this is the very idea the objector is apparently trying to avoid!

So from these three answers, it is clear the objection of inconsistency fails. When God seeks himself as his ultimate end in creating the world, he is being totally consistent with his own unchanging and perfect character.

10
THE OBJECTION OF SELFISHNESS

In this work I have been arguing from the realm of reason that God aims at himself as his own ultimate end in creating the world. In the last chapter, I answered the objection of inconsistency sometimes raised against this conclusion. Here, another objection often presented against these ideas will be addressed:

Objection 2: God would be selfish if he were his own last end.

According to this objection, God simply would not be most interested in his own glory as the main goal he had in mind when he created the world. To do so, the objector says, would be dishonorable to God because it would in effect present God as selfish. It would assume that God engages in all his works in a selfish way.

When we think of human creatures, selfishness is considered miserable and despicable! Man is but a worm of the dust, but even in man a selfish spirit is considered unbecoming and even hateful. We see in man a base and contemptible character, governed by selfish principles in all his activities. He seems to make his own private interests the guiding principle for all his conduct in life.

Thus how can we possible attribute any such spirit to almighty God? That should be the furthest thing from our mind, says the objector! God is the blessed and only potentate! Rather than selfishness, would it not be more fitting for us to ascribe to God the most noble and generous character qualities we can think of? Should we not think of God as having those qualities that are the most remote from anything and everything that is private, narrow, and sordid?

Answer 1: Careless notions of selfishness and generosity

This objection can only arise from an extremely ignorant and careless notion of the vice of selfishness and the virtue of generosity. If the concept of selfishness means that a particular being is inclined to have respect and honor for his own self, this alone does not seem vicious or unbecoming.

Sure, it does seem wrong when the being doesn't seem to realize that one is less than a multitude. That is, the well-being of the public at large should be of greater value to that being than his own self-interest. We created beings think of selfishness more in terms of *group health.* One single person must be considered as much less important when compared to the general public. His interests are very small when compared to the interests of the whole system. Therefore, among created beings, an inclination to prefer one's self more than the whole group is rightly called exceedingly vicious. But it is only considered to be a wicked vice because it doesn't agree with the basic nature of things. Nor does it fit with what will, generally speaking, bring the greatest good.

Likewise, the same is true when a person has the opposite inclination, when he foregoes his own interests for the sake of others. Even though this seems like a virtue among created beings in a group setting, it is not better than simply treating things according to their actual value. Though we call this attitude generosity, it is no more worthy of being called generosity than the attitude which treats things exactly *according to their actual value.* It seems just as virtuous to engage in an action simply because that particular action is most worthy to be engaged in. One might express a preference to something other than self-interest simply because the other thing is worthy in itself to be preferred higher than self-interest.

This is how we think among the community of created beings. But God is not a created being, nor is he part of a group of created beings. God is so great and so excellent that all other beings are like nothing to him (indeed, less than nothing). All of their excellent qualities are vain and empty when compared to his excellent qualities. This obviously makes a major difference when it comes to understanding which actions are virtuous and which are vicious for him.

Additionally, God is omniscient, which means he knows everything there is to know. He is also infallible, which means he never makes any mistakes. Thus he is totally dependable in every way. This being the case, *God knows what sort of being he actually is.* He is most certainly aware that he is the highest and infinitely most valuable being that exists.

If all these things are true of God, and indeed they are, then it is fitting and right for God's heart to be agreeable to these truths, since this is the way things really are, all in their proper proportions. His heart will also be agreeable to his own perfect and all-encompassing understanding of these things. He sees all these truths about himself and the true nature of all things from a perfect point of view and with clear light.

Thus it is most fitting and suitable that God would value himself infinitely more than he values his creatures. It is not in any way viciously selfish for him to do so, considering the type of being he is and knows he is.

Answer 2: Benefit for the general public

There is another way to counter the objection of selfishness. When we think about how created beings in a group work, it is proper to think that one person's self-interest might be set in opposition to the public welfare at large. After all, this person may have private interests that are inconsistent with the public good. In other words, the things the person is interested in may interfere with or oppose the general good of the group. His private interests are in opposition to the public.

But it would be impossible to say the same of God. God is the Supreme Being, the Author and Head of the whole system. In fact, the whole system depends on him. He is the fountain of all being. He is good to the whole. It is most absurd to think that his private interests could somehow be opposed to the interests of the whole system.

To illustrate, think of the natural human body and how it works. It would be absurd to think that the head, heart, and other vital organs could have interests that are opposed to the welfare of the whole body! It is even more absurd to think God could have self-interests that stand in conflict to the system he has created as a whole. Furthermore, it is impossible that God, being omniscient, would ever think of his own interests as being somehow inconsistent with or opposed to the good of the whole.

Answer 3: God's good and the good of his creatures

So far, it has been clearly shown that God is not being wickedly selfish in seeking himself as his last end in the creation of the world. But one other answer should be given to this objection: God's seeking himself in this way is not at all inconsistent with the good of his creatures. In fact, it would be impossible for his seeking himself to be at odds with the good of his creatures, for his self-regard is the very kind of thing that inclines him to seek the good of his creatures.

Why? Because it is his self-honor and self-regard that leads him to spread out his glory and communicate it to other beings. He finds so much wondrous delight within his own internal fullness and glory that he is inclined to pour it out in emanating light. This abundantly flowing glory overwhelms his creatures with good. The same inclination within God that moves him to delight in his glory also causes him to delight in the exhibitions, expressions, and communications of his glory. This is a natural conclusion.

By way of illustration, if there was someone who could not stand the bright light of sunshine, then he would want the sun's bright shining light to be contained within itself. This person's inclination of mind would lead him to see the sun and its shining light as unlovely, so he would wish that this bright light might be trapped and unable to emanate. But this is not true of people who *love* the sun's appearance. They see it as an amiable and glorious thing. Rather than wish its glory was trapped and contained, these people want it to shine brightly, diffusing and spreading itself throughout the whole world. Likewise, those who love God want his glory to shine and flow, and they find great personal benefit when it does!

By the way, some people who write on this subject should perhaps be charged with inconsistency. Whereas, these writers speak out against the doctrine of God making himself his own highest and last end, yet they seem to support human creatures seeking their own happiness as *their* highest end.

As it relates to God, they write that he would be filled with ignoble selfishness to do such a thing. They write this even though God alone is fit to be made the highest end, being the *only one* who deserves such exalted honor to be bestowed upon him, whether he bestows this honor upon himself or those he made bestow it. After all, he is the highest of all beings, infinitely greater and more worthy than all others.

But when it comes to created beings, these same writers maintain that seeking one's own happiness (making it their ultimate end in all they do) is a most virtuous thing to do, and that it should be done necessarily and constantly! They maintain this even though the creature is infinitely less worthy than God to receive supreme and ultimate regard from anybody, including themselves!

They write that when creatures seek their own happiness above all other things, this becomes the foundation for all the other good they can do. They say human creatures should be more concerned with aiming at their own happiness than with aiming at any other virtuous actions they can achieve, even the most virtuous deeds people can do. They do add that when operating by this principle, people should regulate their seeking by wisdom and prudence. But the argument as a whole is obviously inconsistent.

Hopefully, you can see that the objection of selfishness in God fails, just as the prior objection of inconsistency fails. But we are not finished analyzing objections. Next we will show the weaknesses of the objection of unworthiness.

11
THE OBJECTION OF UNWORTHINESS

In this chapter we continue Section IV (analyzing objections). Keep in mind, we are still working only within the realm of reason. Once we finish analyzing the final two objections, we will move into the second major division of this work. There we will focus mainly on what the Word of God has to say about these things.

Now we have the task of analyzing and critiquing the third objection commonly brought against the notion that God aimed at himself and his glory as his own last end in creating the world.

Objection 3: It would be unworthy of God to seek delight from his creatures.

This objection can be explained like this: If God does make himself his own end, then this seems to be unworthy of God. Why? Because if God makes himself his own final end, then he is striving to make his own glory and excellent perfection known. This means he would be seeking the love, esteem, and delight of his creatures as they see his glory and perfections. But, asks the objector, can this be something a worthy God would do?

The objector might further explain that, on a human level, a truly great man doesn't allow himself to be overly influenced in his actions by the applause of people, not even a great crowd of people. It is below him to be swayed by such a thing. Neither the prince nor the philosopher would aim toward such a low end. They do not engage in their important activities, great and noble enterprises, for such a meaningless purpose.

Thus it would be all the more unworthy for the great God to perform his magnificent works for such a low end. It doesn't seem to make sense, states the objector, that God would create the vast universe because he wanted the notice and admiration of minuscule worms of the dust. God is infinitely higher than all the creatures he has made. Why then would he seek their praise and applause?

When we think of classes of human creatures, it is obvious that the greatest prince and the greatest philosopher are much higher than the ordinary mobs of people. But God is infinitely higher than the greatest prince and the greatest philosopher! So why would he care if these small creatures gaze at his displays of magnificence? Why would he care if the worms of the dirt clap their hands for his beauty?

It should be admitted that this objection does seem to have some strength on the surface. But truly it is only an appearance of strength. Once the arguments are considered more closely, they will be shown erroneous and unfounded.

Answer 1: Valuing the most valuable thing

This objection pertains to the worthiness of God in relationship to what he values. Is it worthy of God or not to value what is truly excellent in itself? Is it worthy of God or not to regard, respect, and find pleasure in the existence of something that has infinite value and excellent qualities innate in itself?

The following proposition seems to be true without liability to doubt: Prior to creation, *some future existence* was valuable and worthy to be brought into being. If not, God would not have created anything at all, for he would have had nothing worthy to desire or seek and so nothing worthy to be made his end in creation.

Prior to creation, if there was any future thing that was fit and valuable in itself, I think it must be the knowledge of God's glory, along with the esteem and love of it. After all, the highest kind of created existence is understanding and will. If these two things are valuable, then their value must be in their exercise.

Furthermore, *the highest and most excellent way* of exercising understanding and will is in having actual knowledge and in the actual exercise of the will. And certainly the most excellent actual knowledge and willing in the creature is knowledge of God and the willingness to love him. Additionally, the highest *type* of actual, excellent knowledge of God is the knowledge of his glory or moral excellence. And the highest type of *actually exercising the will* consists in esteeming, loving, and delighting in God's glory.

If anything in creation is worthy in itself to exist – such as this high understanding and exercise of the will – then such a communication from God of his divine glory to the creature is also worthy of existence. Likewise, if there was a time when this knowledge of God and the ability to will in this highest way did not exist, then the same conclusion holds. God was worthy to bring this communication of his divine glory into existence so that the creatures he made could possess this highest type of knowledge and exercise their wills in this highest way.

On the other hand, if there was no future thing prior to creation that was worthy to exist, then God would have had no future thing to aim at in his creating the world. But if nothing was worthy to be aimed at in creation, then nothing was worthy to be God's end in creation. He would have had no reason to create anything.

But God did have a purpose in his creation. Since his excellent qualities and glory are worthy to be highly valued and delighted in, then God is worthy when he himself values and delights in them. He is further worthy when he communicates his divine fullness to the creatures he made. And he is worthy when he is aware of the esteem and praise that they give to him because they see and treasure his excellent qualities and glory; he is worthy when he values these things. This is a necessary conclusion.

For the sake of clarity, consider the following illustration. Think of how it is when we regard the excellent qualities of another person. Suppose we place great value in proper proportion on the virtues and excellent qualities of a friend. When we do, we will also quite naturally approve of and enjoy the esteem that other people give to our friend. On the flip side, we will disapprove of any contempt other people might show to our friend. Indeed, we will disdain such behavior! If the virtues possessed by our friend are truly valuable, then it is worthy for us show approval when others esteem our friend's virtues. Likewise, it is worthy to show disapproval when others display contempt for them.

The same is true for a being who is considering his own qualities and attributes. If he truly admires them and takes great delight in them, then he will also (naturally and necessarily) love occasions when other people do as well. Similarly, he will disdain it when they show contempt for these qualities and attributes.

Furthermore, what if the attributes this being has are *truly worthy* of be greatly admired in reality? Then indeed, the being who has them is also worthy in a proportioned way to show approval to the esteem given to him by other beings. This is a point that everyone should consider very well.

Is it right for God to be pleased when others hold him in contempt? Is it fitting that he be joyful when his created beings despise him? Of course not! To the contrary, it is fitting and proper for God to be *displeased* when his created beings hold him in contempt and despise him. But this also means that it is fitting and proper for him to be *pleased* when proper love, esteem, and honor are given to him.

This point can be further illuminated when we consider what it is about our nation that leads to our approval. What is it about our nation that we place value on? Certainly, it is becoming of us to love our country. The qualities of our nation give rise to our properly proportioned esteem and praise of it. So obviously we should also place value on those occasions when other people also give proper honor to our country.

What is right and fitting for us to seek for our friend and for our country is also right and fitting for God to seek for himself. If we value our friend's excellent qualities and the honor given to him by others and if we value our nation and the honor given to it by others, then God should also love and value himself and the honor given to him by others. I think this point has already been proven.

Now, let me call your attention to two important thoughts. First, within the being of God, the love he has for himself and the love he has for the public are not separated and distinguished, as it is in man. This is because God's being is such that it comprehends all. God exists infinitely, so his existence is the equivalent of universal existence. Thus for the same reason that it is fit and beautiful for humans to have affection for the public, God's regard and value for himself is also fit and beautiful.

Secondly, within the being of God, his love for virtue – that which is fit and decent – cannot be separated from the love he has for himself. This is because loving God is primarily and chiefly what makes up all virtue and holiness. So God's own holiness must also primarily consist in the love he has for himself, as we have already seen. If God's holiness consists in the love he has for himself, then this implies that God approves of and is pleased with the esteem and love that others give him as well. After all, a being who loves himself will necessarily love when love is given to him. For if God's love to himself is what constitutes his holiness, then the love that created beings have for God is what constitutes *their* holiness. And if God loves holiness in himself, then he must also love it in the beings he has created.

The latest most seemingly reputable philosophers understand virtue as being found in a person's affection for the public or in his general goodwill towards others. If this is where the primary essence of virtue is found, then what virtue is there in loving virtue itself? The only virtue of loving virtue itself can come if it is implied in or arises from this public affection or from an extensive goodwill of mind. This is true because if a man truly loves the public, then he also necessarily loves when *love is shown* to the public. For the same reason, having a love for virtue itself is virtuous only as it is implied in or arises from love for the divine being. This is the case if universal goodwill in the highest sense is the same thing as having goodwill toward the divine being, who is in effect universal being.

Consequently, God's love for himself implies also a love of virtue. Furthermore, God's love of virtue is itself virtuous only because it arises from the love he has for himself. This means God's virtuous character and inclination, which appears in his love for the holiness of his created beings, is to be understood as the same thing as the love God has for himself. And this means that whenever God makes virtue his end, he makes himself his end.

To summarize, since God is an all-comprehending being, then all of his moral perfections are to be resolved, in one way or another, into a supreme and infinite regard for himself. His moral perfections include his holiness, justice, grace, and benevolence, among others. If this is so, then it is easy to see why it suits God perfectly to make himself his own supreme and last end in all his works.

By the way, observe another inconsistency some people might hold. Imagine an objector holding the following positions. First, he insists that God could only love and take delight in the virtue of his creatures for the sake of the virtue itself and not in any way loving the virtue out of an ultimate love for himself. Second, the objector insists that God would be much too selfish if we supposed that all of his delight in virtue should be understood as an ultimate delight in himself.

If someone attempted to hold both of these positions, then he would be contradicting an objection that was raised earlier. That objection says that God does not take pleasure in communicating himself to others and that God is perfectly independent and self-sufficient, so all his happiness and pleasure is found in the enjoyment of himself. But in this present objection, the objector insists that it is becoming for God to have pleasure, love, and delight *in virtue itself* for its own sake and in a manner that is distinct from the delight he has for himself. So if the same person attempts to make both objections, he will be inconsistent with himself.

Answer 2: Grace leads to honor

Let us now consider another answer to the objection of unworthiness, which says that it would be unworthy of God to seek the esteem and love of his creatures since they are infinitely inferior to him. To the contrary, I would observe that it is not unworthy at all for God to take pleasure in something that is in itself fitting and amiable, even if he finds it in those that are infinitely below him. Even if it requires God to show infinite grace and condescension, yet this is still not unworthy of God, but rather honors and glorifies him in an infinite way.

When people insist that God's own glory was not an ultimate end for him in creating the world, they give the impression that they are exalting and magnifying God's benevolence and love for his creatures. After all, they suppose all that God had in mind was the happiness of his creatures, so he made them his last end and not himself. He had no regard for himself, they maintain, but only for the creature. To those who hold this view, it makes God seem more loving and benevolent.

But those who object this way are being inconsistent. They seem to maintain, on the one hand, that it would be unworthy for God to be interested in seeking the love and praise of people. But then, on the other hand, they also seem to maintain that God so highly values people, his love for them being so great, that he makes *them* his last end and not himself. But it is inconsistent to hold both of these views at the same time.

It is in the very nature of love – especially a great love – that the one who is giving love will value the returned adoration of the person he loves. So it will give God pleasure when his people show proper love and esteem for him. This follows from both God's love for himself and his love to his creatures. If he highly values and loves himself, he must also approve when others highly value and love him. Likewise, he must disapprove when they do not. Similarly, if God loves and values his creatures, he must take delight and find value in their mutual love for him and when they place high value upon him. He delights when they delight in him *precisely because he loves them* and not because he somehow needs them.

Answer 3: The value of wise and just esteem

Part of the objection of unworthiness says that the great men among us do not govern their behavior by the applause of the masses of people who are beneath their dignity. The objector maintains that if it is below dignified human beings to do this, then certainly it is unworthy of God as well.

But consider the following observation: The problem with the applause of the multitude is that it is usually given in ignorance. Frequently, the masses give praise to dignified people without any real understanding of things. People have a strong tendency to operate on a level of giddiness and injustice, and they give their applause on the shaky ground of these things. They often do not have a reasonable or just view of things, operating out of error, folly, and unreasonable emotions. Of course, this type of applause should truly be disregarded.

However, it is not beneath a dignified and wise man to value the esteem of others, even others who are inferior to him, if their esteem for him is wise and just. If this dignified person did despise their wise and just applause, it would not show at all that he had a great mind, but rather that he was haughty and had a mean spirit!

God has a regard only for the wise praise and just esteem that people have for him. He is not at all interested in an ignorant and unjust type of applause and praise. Furthermore, wise and just esteem for God is the only type that is truly fitting and valuable in itself.

Hopefully, it has been clearly shown that the objection of unworthiness fails along with the first two objections. But there is one more objection that must be faced.

12
THE OBJECTION OF FREENESS AND OBLIGATION

The key argument made in this work is that God's main reason for creating the world was himself. He made himself his own ultimate end when he brought created things into being. We have been showing how reason and rational thought support this argument well.

We've also been considering the reality that many people object to this argument. The first three of these objections have already been analyzed and were shown to be weak and lacking. In fact, they fail in any significant way to harm the idea that God made himself his own last end in creating the world. In this chapter we will consider the fourth and final of these objections:

Objection 4: Divine freeness and creaturely obligation would be in jeopardy if God were his own last end.

Some would object by saying this would take away from the freeness of God's goodness. The objector worries that God's freedom to show kindness and generosity to his creatures would be jeopardized if he created the world for his own glory.

In addition, this objection maintains that God's created beings have an *obligation to show gratitude* to him for the good things he communicates to them. This obligation is slighted, so they say, if God created the world for his own ultimate sake. The objector explains that if God, in communicating his fullness, makes himself his end, then everything he does is for himself, not for his created beings. He does it all for his own sake, not theirs. The objector wonders how this can be free love and how the created beings can be expected to respond in gratitude. After all, what God has done was not ultimately done *for them.*

Answer 1: Not at odds

But God and his creatures are not to be thought of as set in opposition to one another when it comes to the spreading emanation of God's divine fullness. They are not the opposite parts of a disjunction. Similarly, neither should the glory of God and the good of the creature be spoken of like they are properly and entirely distinct from one another. This objection makes the mistake of assuming these things must be totally separate and distinct.

The objector speaks like this: If God respects and loves his own glory, then he simply cannot also communicate good to his creatures. Or: If God communicates his fullness for the purpose of his own glory, then he cannot be communicating it in any way for the benefit of his creatures. The objection erroneously holds that God can't do both, since it is assumed that these things stand in opposition. But actually these things do not stand in opposition nor are they entirely distinct, as they may appear to be.

This truth would appear more clearly to us if we had the capability of seeing the bigger picture of God and the divine things he is doing. If our view of these things, which are so much higher than we are, was fuller and more perfect, we would see that God's glory and the good of the creature are not opposed at all. Rather, they are implied in each other.

God is seeking after his own glory. This is reality, pure and simple. His glory is his ultimate end. But *within* his seeking his own glory, he is seeking the good of his creatures as well. We know this is true because the shining emanation of his glory communicates his excellent qualities to the creature. *It is the source of their happiness.* Indeed, God seeks after and delights in this glorious shining emanation in the same way that he delights in himself and his own eternal glory.

So as he is communicating his fullness to the creature, which benefits them tremendously, he does it ultimately for himself. The good of the creature is found when they are in union and communion with him. God *is* their good. When the creature displays excellent qualities and happiness, this is nothing more than the expressions of God's glory shining in and through them. Thus in seeking their glory and happiness, God ultimately seeks himself. And as he seeks himself (that is, himself diffused and shining outwardly, which he delights in just as he delights in his innate beauty and fullness), he seeks their glory and happiness as well.

This doctrine shines more clearly when we consider the *degree* of excellent qualities and happiness God desires for the creature. In creating the world, God had in mind the fullness of his design plan for the world from beginning to end. This design plan is *eternal* in duration. So the degree of glory and happiness his creatures experience, as they draw closer and closer to him in ever increasing measure, is constantly growing throughout all of eternity.

Likewise, the doctrine shines even more clearly when we think of the *manner* in which God brings about their glory and happiness. He does it through the process of bringing the creature closer to himself. Throughout all eternity, as his design plan for the world unfolds, God moves his people into stricter union with himself. In this communion with God, the creatures participate more and more in his glory and happiness.

God had this full view of the creature's good in mind when he made the world. He saw the big picture, the entire eternal duration of his design plan. Before creating he viewed both the degree and manner of the glory and good of his creatures. He observed and understood their eternal progressive union and communion with him. Because this is the way God sees it, then *it is the way it truly is*. God's people must be viewed as being in infinite and strict union with him. Thus when we look at the larger picture as God does, it appears clear that God's love and respect for the creature unites with the love and respect he has for himself.

To illustrate, think of two lines, one representing God's seeking his own glory and the other representing God seeking the good of the creature. At first it seems these two lines are separate. But as it turns out, they are aiming to finally meet one another. They are both directed towards the same center. When we remember that the good of the creature must be viewed in its entire duration as an infinite progression, then we see the line that represents their good not only as a communication of God's glory, but as coming nearer and nearer to the same thing in its infinite fullness. The closer anything comes to infinite, the closer it comes to an identity with God. If something is good as viewed by God, and he beholds it as infinite, then it cannot be viewed as something distinct from God's own infinite glory.

The apostle Paul in Ephesians discusses the great love Christ has for men. As we read we are led to think that the love Christ has for his church coincides with his love for himself. This is because of the strict union the church has with him. For example:

> **Ephesians 5:25-30** Husbands, love your wives, as Christ loved the church and gave himself up for her. . . so that he might present the church to himself in splendor. . . In the same way husbands should love their wives as their own bodies. He who loves his wife loves himself. . . just as Christ does the church, because we are members of his body.

We are of his "flesh" and of his "bones," as Paul's reference to Genesis 2:23-24 implies. As I understand this passage, there is nothing in God's seeking the good of his creatures or in his desire to communicate his own fullness to them that detracts in any way from the excellence of his glorious fullness. Nor do I see anything here that would detract from the creature's obligation to be grateful to God for it.

Now, the communication of God's goodness is not something less than God's goodness itself. Just because it is a flowing, outward communication of his glory does not mean that it is any less than his innate glory, properly speaking. This is because the good he is communicating is something of himself. Thus he delights in it just as he delights in his own glory, properly speaking.

Likewise, the creature's benefit in this overflowing glory of God is not less just because it is a flowing type of communication. Neither is this overflowing, communicated glory lessened in its direct tendency to provide benefit to the creature or to love the creature when he comes to exist. It operates the same as God's own inner glory does.

Furthermore, the inclination within God to communicate and spread his goodness outward is not somehow less excellent simply because it arises out of his love and respect for himself. This is because the love he has for himself implies nothing more than the reality that God loves whatever is most worthy and excellent. The outwardly flowing emanation of God's glory is, in itself, most worthy and excellent, so God delights in it as an ultimate end, not as a means to some further end. The delight he has in this excellent emanation extends from the love that he has for himself in his own fullness. After all, he is the fountain, the sum, and the whole of everything that is excellent.

These are the facts of the matter, and that is why this objection fails along with the others. The supposed problems raised in the object can't detract from the excellent nature of God's inclination to emanate his own glory and fullness or from the communication of good to his creatures.

Answer 2: Possible inconsistencies not applicable to God

God's inclination to communicate his goodness in this manner (from self-regard and delight in his own glory) does not diminish at all the freeness of his goodwill towards the creatures. This is clear if we consider carefully the possible ways doing good to others out of the motive of self-love *might* be inconsistent with the freeness of goodwill. I can think of only two ways they may be inconsistent with each other.

The first goes like this: If someone does a good deed for another out of a confined self-love, this is considered the *opposite* of having a general goodwill towards others. In fact, this kind of self-love is properly called *selfishness*.

But in some sense, the most benevolent and generous person in the world is seeking his own happiness as he seeks to do good for others. How can this be? Because he places his happiness *in their good.* In a manner of speaking, his mind is large enough that he takes them into himself. Thus when they are happy, he feels it too. He partakes with them in their happiness, so that when they are made happy, he is happy. In no way is this inconsistent with his free desire to benefit them. On the contrary, his free benevolence and kindness is made up of this kind of happiness-seeking. The highest freedom people can have in doing good to others comes out of this general benevolence and love for other beings, not from some confined selfishness.

Apply this thinking to God. He is a divine being that has no such thing as confined selfishness in him. His love for himself is not somehow opposite to his general goodwill towards the creature. That would be impossible, because he comprehends all existence and everything that is excellent as in his own essence.

Think about it. God is the *first being*. As the eternal, infinite first being, he is in effect *being in general*. Nothing else can be without him being first. As being in general, God continually comprehends everything that exists universally, a point that has already been made. Since he is being in general, and nothing else exists independently of him, then God is not the kind of being who could enlarge his heart by showing benevolence to the creatures he has made. That is, if by enlarging his heart we mean he takes them into himself and is somehow benefited by them. How could a divine being do that? Why would he who is distinct and independent take into himself that which originally came out of him? This simply can't be for an infinite being who alone exists from eternity.

But in another manner of speaking, when God shows his goodness to the creatures, he does enlarge himself in a more excellent and divine way. He does this by communicating and spreading his glory outward to the creature. He does not find creatures and show them goodness so that he can take them into himself, partake of their good, and be happy in them. This would not be fitting for an eternal being that is totally independent of the creature. Rather by flowing forth his light and glory and expressing himself to them and in them, *he makes them partake of him*. He then rejoices in himself as expressed in them. He delights in his perfect attributes and glory communicated to them.

The second potential way that doing good from the motive of self-love might be inconsistent with the freeness of benevolence can be seen in the following idea: Doing good to others from self-love implies that the benefactor is somehow dependent upon those to whom he is doing good. It is as if the one doing good is only doing so because of a need or desire, and he is depending on the object of his goodness to supply and satisfy that need or desire. In this type of case, showing goodwill towards others doesn't happen because the benefactor is self-moved. It happens because he is constrained to do so by something outside himself, namely, his dependence upon the ones to whom he is doing good.

But when it comes to God, this problem fades away. God, in making himself his own last end in the way that has been described, does not show any dependence at all upon the creatures to whom he is working good. Rather, with God it is totally consistent with his absolute independence and self-sufficiency. There is something in God's inclination to communicate goodness that also shows him to be absolutely independent and totally self-moved in it. He does this in a way that is unique to him and above the way creatures show good to one another.

Yes, created human beings can be very gracious and kind to each other. But even the most gracious and kind of them are not independent or self-moved in their goodness. Rather, in every act of goodwill towards another, the creature is motivated by some object that they find. Something appears to them that they consider good or in some way worthy of respect, and this is what moves their kindness.

It is not so with God. He, all alone, is absolutely self-moved. This being the case, when he desires to communicate the fullness of his glory, he does so from absolutely within himself. He is not motivated by something in the object or by anything else. This is because all that is good and worthy in the object (indeed the very existence of the object) comes from him! If any object exists and is worthy to be praised and valued, then its existence and worthiness is ultimately an overflow of his goodness. God alone stands in this kind of relationship to the created order. Thus he is absolutely and only self-moved when it comes to showing goodwill towards others.

This analysis shows that, when we suppose that God made himself his own last end in the way described, it does not at all diminish the obligation of his created beings to show proper gratitude to him. His creatures have received wonderful communications from him, so they should be truly thankful.

If God's having made himself his own last end in creation does lessen the obligation of his created beings to be thankful, it does so for one of the following reasons. First, the creature has not benefited that much by it. Second, it is not flowing from an inclination towards proper goodness, in which case it would not have such a direct tendency to benefit the creature. Third, the inclination in God to communicate his goodness is not truly the kind of thing that is virtuous and excellent. Fourth, it might be that the goodwill given by God to the creatures is not freely given.

But clearly none of these things take place. All the points I have made demonstrate this. God's inclination to communicate the fullness of himself, which is the inclination that we are supposing motivated God to create the world, is not tainted by any of these four reasons. Thus, this objection fails along with the others.

END OF FIRST DIVISION

This brings to conclusion the first major division of this work. We have carefully considered what reason teaches us regarding the matter of God making himself his own last end. Additionally, we demonstrated the errors of the four major objections brought against this doctrine.

At this conclusion I must make a confession. When we look so closely and consider so carefully these subjects, there is a degree of indistinctness and obscurity. Additionally, I realize there is a great imperfection regarding the expressions we use concerning these matters. But this arises unavoidably from the nature of what we are studying. There is an infinite sublimity to it and an incomprehensibleness that always comes with thinking about things divine.

Since this is the case, God's revelation is the surest guide in thinking through these matters. In the next chapter, we will begin the second major division of the work. There we will consider what God's sure revelation, the Word of God, teaches about the issues that are before us.

Nevertheless, the material covered in this first division is very helpful. We have endeavored to listen careful to the voice of reason and discover what it says. Reason, however, can only go so far. But as far as it does go, it may serve to prepare the way by removing the objections so many people insist on.

Furthermore, it is not against reason at all to consider what the Word of God says about this matter and be satisfied by it. So listening to reason and listening to the Word of God are not at odds with one another in the least. Indeed, listening to reason may prepare our minds to more fully accept the instructions given to us in the Word of God. What we have learned from reason may also help us to interpret the words and expressions often found in the Bible about this subject in a more natural and genuine sense. To the Word of God we now turn.

13
Second Division: What Scripture Teaches

We have endeavored in the first major division of this work to consider what reason teaches us about why God made the world. The proposed conclusion is abundantly supported by reason, namely, that God made himself his own ultimate end in creating the world. And further, that God's desire to benefit his creatures is in no way inconsistent with his ultimate end. No objection raised against these truths can stand, as has been clearly shown.

It is now time to turn to the Holy Scriptures. What can be deduced from reason and what the Bible teaches on this matter are not at odds in any way. It will be shown in the following chapters that reason and the Bible both lead us to the exact same place.

This major division, like the first, is broken into various sections which build upon one another. There are seven sections here, and it will be helpful for you to see them together as a whole before we consider them individually.

SECTION I: Basic overview

SECTION II: Some interpretive positions

SECTION III: Scriptural demonstrations of God's glory as his ultimate end in creating the world

SECTION IV: For the sake of his name, so that his perfections will be known, and so that he will be praised

SECTION V: The communication of good to his creatures as an ultimate end

SECTION VI: A consideration of the biblical phrases "glory of God" and "name of God"

SECTION VII: Only one ultimate end and what it is

We proceed now to consider each of these sections in careful detail.

Section I: Basic overview

When we read the Scriptures, they clearly show on all occasions that God makes himself his own end in all his works, which must include his work of creating the world. The same being who is the first cause of all things is also presented as the supreme and last end of all things.

Here is a survey of passages from the books of Isaiah and Revelation that make this point. Notice the *first and last* language that the Lord uses to identify himself in each of these verses:

> **Isaiah 44:6** Thus says the LORD, the King of Israel and his Redeemer, the LORD of hosts: "I am the first and I am the last; besides me there is no god."
>
> **Isaiah 48:12** Listen to me, O Jacob, and Israel, whom I called! I am he; I am the first, and I am the last.
>
> **Revelation 1:8; 11; 17** I am the Alpha and the Omega. . . who is and who was and who is to come, the Almighty. . . I am the Alpha and the Omega, the first and the last (KJV). . . I am the first and the last.
>
> **Revelation 21:6** He said to me, "It is done! I am the Alpha and the Omega, the beginning and the end."
>
> **Revelation 22:13** I am the Alpha and the Omega, the first and the last, the beginning and the end.

It is important to observe how God is referred to in these verses as both the first *and the last*. He is both the beginning *and the end*. What is meant or at least implied is that just as God is the first efficient cause of all things, he is also the final object for which they are made. As to being the first, God is the fountain of all being. All things spring from and originate with him. As to being the last, all things are moving towards God as their ultimate end goal. When we carefully analyze these passages, this seems to be the most natural understanding of the expressions we read. This interpretation is further confirmed by the following parallel passages:

> **Romans 11:36** For from him and through him and to him are all things.
>
> **Colossians 1:16** For by him all things were created, in heaven and on earth, visible and invisible, whether thrones or dominions or rulers or authorities - all things were created through him and for him.
>
> **Hebrews 2:10** For it was fitting that he, for whom and by whom all things exist.
>
> **Proverbs 16:4** The LORD hath made all things for himself. (KJV)

Notice, especially in the last verse, how direct and specific the language is. According to these passages, it is evident why God is considered the last end, to whom and for whom all things exist. It is truly fitting and suitable for him to stand at the beginning and at the end of all things. This reality is a branch of God's glory. He is positioned in the proper place for an eternal being who is so great and infinite. Thus it is appropriate for us to think of God in this dignified way; after all, he is infinitely above all other beings. Every other being is a created being that exists and is sustained only by his power. In comparison with God, all other things are as nothing.

These preliminary considerations move us now into Section II.

Section II: Some interpretive positions

From the passages just seen, the Scriptures in general state that God makes himself his own ultimate end, both when he created the world and in all his works. But there is a question that we must now ask and answer: When teaching that God makes himself his own end, how do the Scriptures represent this?

For example, it is evident that God doesn't make his own existence the end of his creation. His being itself cannot be the thing he is aiming at in creation, nor could we imagine such a thing, it is utterly absurd. God's being and existence must be in place prior to any of his acts or designs. Without presupposing his being and existence, there is no ground for any of his actions. A non-existent being can't do anything! Therefore, it can't be in this sense that God makes himself his end in creating the world. It is totally illogical to say that God created the world so that he might have existence.

Neither does it make sense to say that God created the world so that he might have certain attributes, perfections, or a particular essence. No passage in the Scriptures gives even the slightest impression that this is how we are to understand God making himself his ultimate end.

So what do the Scriptures mean to teach us about this issue? What is the thing (divine effect) that, in relation to himself, God was aiming at in his works of creation? When he designed the world, in what way exactly did God make himself his own ultimate end?

In order to help us keep a right understanding of the scriptural teaching on this issue, I lay down the following positions. These positions are designed to help us draw correct inferences from biblical passages that relate to this matter. Hopefully, they will help open the way to a true and definitive answer to the questions above.

Position 1: God's ultimate end for his works of providence in general is the same as his ultimate end for all of creation.

When we read the Bible, we find many passages that refer to God's general works of providence. These passages speak of the way God sovereignly guides the course of history (especially human history), broadly speaking. When we study these verses carefully, we can discern what God's ultimate end is in relation to these general works of providence. It seems abundantly clear that whatever his ultimate end relative to his general works of providence, it is exactly that same end that he has in mind for his entire work of creation as a whole. These cannot be different ends.

This important issue has already been discussed (See Page 28, Point H), and I do not need to repeat it here.

Position 2: God's ultimate end can be discerned from passages that mention only some of God's works of providence.

This position relates to those parts of the Scriptures where a particular thing is mentioned as God's ultimate end in relation to only some of his works. Under Position 1, we discussed God's providential guidance of all things in a general sense, but sometimes the Scriptures mention a particular thing as the end goal God had in mind with only some of his works. In other words, they are much narrower in their scope of observation.

In these particular cases, we must study the context of the passage carefully. If we see God engaging in a work and his end goal for that work is mentioned, we must observe whether that goal is the same one that God has in mind for all his other works. If it is the same goal, then we are right to infer that this particular effect is a last end to all of God's other works as well. This is true even if the passage does not directly mention all his other works.

However, when considering whether this thing is the end of God's other works, care must be taken in our analysis. We must ask the following of the effect cause by God's working: Does it have a peculiar beauty and value about it? Does this beauty and value fit only with the work mentioned in the passage, or does it fit the broader end of what God is doing with all his works in general?

In other words, if this thing has a peculiar fit to be the last end of *only the specific works of God mentioned in the passage,* then it must not be inferred that this particular thing is the ultimate end of all of God's works generally. But barring any such peculiarity, we are just to infer that the thing is the proper ultimate end of the specific works of God mentioned in the passage *as well as all of God's works generally,* even if they are not directly mentioned in the passage.

Why would we make such an inference? Because of the high value of the effect (or end product of God's work) itself. This is exactly why God makes it the end of those works that are expressly mentioned in the passage. Furthermore, the effect produced is equal with the work itself in terms of value, since it results from the work. So it makes good sense to say that the effect is the natural consequence – or last end – of the particular works of God taken as a set, whether the ones directly mentioned in the passage or all of God's works generally speaking.

Position 3: God's ultimate end can be discerned from frequent mention.

It is safe to assume that God, in his desire to communicate his Word accurately to people, would be insistent in identifying his ultimate end for creating the world. After all, his ultimate end for creating the world is also his ultimate end for all his works of providence (as we saw earlier) and in the highest sense. Indeed, God's ultimate end is more important than anything else at all.

Therefore, as we study the Bible and its account of God's designs and ends in his works of providence, we should be careful to notice those things that are most frequently mentioned. If something in particular is mentioned more regarding God's ultimate aim in his works of providence, then we should presume that this thing is the ultimate end of all God's works in general. Thus it is also the ultimate end he had in mind for creating the world.

Position 4: God's ultimate end for the moral system is the same as his ultimate end for all of creation.

Whatever the Scriptures teach as God's last end with respect to the moral system, this is also his last end in his work of creation in general. God's aim in the creation and governing of the intelligent part of the created system and in the moral government of the world must also be the last end he had in mind for creating the world as a whole. This point is evident as we observe the constitution of the world itself and when we study the Word of God.

But why should we believe that the intelligent, moral part of creation is connected in this way to all of God's works in general? Because the moral part of creation is the end of *all the rest of creation.* In other words, the inanimate, unintelligent parts of creation were made for the benefit of the rational creatures who have knowledge of morality. In the same way, a house is built for the benefit of an inhabitant, not as a mere end in itself.

Further, both reason and the Word of God confirm that moral agents were made in order to carry out what is moral within them. Simply put, the world was made as a place for them to live out their morality. So whatever is the last end for the moral part of creation is also the last end for the rest of creation. It is the reason the rest of the world was made, and thus it is the last end of the whole.

To illustrate, consider the relationship of the hand of a watch to the watch as a whole. If the entire watch was made for the benefit of the hand (to move it properly and to regulate its movement), then it follows that the last end of the hand is also the last end of the whole watch. Moral, intelligent creatures parallel the hand of the watch, while all of creation parallels the watch as a whole. If all of creation exists as a theatre for intelligent creatures to live morally, then all of creation and all morally-capable beings have the exact same ultimate end in God's eyes.

Position 5: God's ultimate end for his most significant works of providence is the same as his ultimate end for all of creation.

As we read the Bible, we can determine God's chief and most important works of providence. As he carries out his plans in the world, these are his most significant works in the process. We must carefully discern what his last end is in these chief works. When we do, we can safely assume that his ultimate end for them is the same ultimate end he had in mind for creating the world as a whole.

This is true because we rightly determine the end of a thing by what it is used for, a point that we've already made. We determine the end of a clock, chariot, ship, or boat motor from the main way it is used.

Apply this thinking to God's providence. *His providence is essentially his use of the world he has made.* If we can determine God's main work (or set of works) of providence, then we can rightly infer from this the main way God uses his creation. From his use we can determine what God had in mind as his ultimate end.

When we take Position 4 and Position 5 together, we infer Position 6:

Position 6: God's ultimate end for his most significant works of providence in the moral world is the same as his ultimate end for all of creation.

Under Position 4, we learned that God's ultimate end for the moral world is the same as his ultimate end for all of creation. Since the moral part of his creation is the most significant part he created, it must also be the ultimate end he had in mind for everything he made. Under Position 5, we learned that God's most important works of providence are done for the same ultimate end as his work of creation as a whole. Remember, the main use God has for his creation indicates what his final end was in making it at all.

Now, let's combine these two positions together. When we read the Bible, sometimes we observe a work of God that can be considered one of his chief works *within the moral world.* So it is both a chief work, and it takes place within the realm of the intelligent, moral beings God has created. When we see this type of passage, we are right to infer from it that whatever God's ultimate end was in that particular work, it is the exact same ultimate end he had in mind for creating the world as a whole.

> *Position 7:* God's ultimate end in the part of the moral world that is good is the same as his ultimate end for all of creation.

Now, we will focus our attention not only on the moral part of world, but on the *good part* of the moral world. After all, there are intelligent, moral beings who are good, and there are plenty who are bad. Whatever the Scriptures teach to be God's last end in relation to the good part, it is the very same last end God had in mind when he created the world as a whole.

How do we infer this? In the context of this discussion, *good* means that which is according to the mind of God. Things are good when they are as God would have them be or when they function as God designed them to function. Thus the good part of the moral world is actually functioning as God desires. This means their lives are aimed towards the end God had in mind when he made them. As goodness exists within them and as they act out their goodness, God's ultimate end is being obtained. So whatever their end goal is must be the same end goal God had in mind when he created all things.

To clarify, we have already established that God created all things for the sake of the moral world. The world exists primarily as a place for the moral realm to exist. But when we zoom into the moral world, we find that *it* exists for the sake of its good part. After all, what is the goodness of a thing? The goodness of a thing consists in its ability to answer its end. It is good if it does what it is designed for or, at least, when it is demonstrating goodness in the eyes of its author. For the author goodness means that the thing he created agrees with what he had in mind for it. It must achieve the purpose for which he made it. If it does, then it is good.

In the case of God creating the moral world, his chief end for intelligent, moral beings is in his mind. Thus moral agents are considered good when they match what he has in mind. When God made moral agents, he designed them to be and do certain things. God considers them good when they achieve these goals he has for them.

In the same way, machines are considered good if they can actually achieve the end for which they were designed. Likewise, instruments and utensils are good if they accomplish their designed purpose. Consequently, if we can determine the chief end someone has in mind when he prepares a utensil to be a good utensil (to function as designed), then we can also determine the chief end of the whole utensil, general speaking.

Take that same understanding and apply it to moral agents. When God creates a moral agent, he has an ultimate end in mind as he prepares him to be a good moral agent (to function according to his design). Whatever that ultimate end is must also be God's ultimate end for creating the moral world as a whole.

Position 8: God's ultimate end for the moral code of conduct give to his moral agents is the same as his ultimate end for all of creation.

When we read the Word of God, we find God giving certain dictates that require his moral agents to behave a certain way. Their conduct is to be regulated by his commands. Thus God's commands are the ultimate and highest end of the moral part of creation.

This means we have strong reason to believe that whatever the Word of God requires moral agents to seek after as their ultimate end, it is the exact same ultimate end God had in mind for them when he created them. Furthermore, on the basis of Position 4, this is also the exact same ultimate end God had for creating the world as a whole.

Consider one of the major differences between the intelligent, moral part of the world and the rest of the world. The intelligent, moral part is actually capable of *knowing* their Creator and the reason he made them. They are capable of actively complying with their creative design, and they can choose to promote this design in their lives. Other creatures cannot do this. They merely comply with the Creator's design only passively and eventually.

Seeing that these intelligent, moral agents are capable of knowing the reason their Author has made them, it is obvious that they have a *duty* to follow his design plan. Their wills should comply with the will of their Creator. They should chiefly seek as their ultimate end the very same thing that God seeks as their ultimate end.

When God reveals his law in the Bible, it agrees with the law of nature regarding the moral agents he has created. God's will as Lawgiver and his will as Creator must agree. Certainly, both the law and nature agree concerning the code of conduct moral agents are to abide by. Thus we conclude that whatever God commands his moral agents to do as revealed in Scripture, this is their ultimate end. God designed them to obey his law, and they are functioning as designed when they do.

Therefore, when we take all the positions covered so far together, we find that God's ultimate goal for providing a code of conduct to the moral part of his creation is the exact same ultimate goal he had in mind for creating the world as a whole. From this we learn that the law portions of Scripture are extremely helpful in determining an answer to our overall question: Why did God create the world?

Position 9: God's ultimate end for the goodness in the good part of the moral world is the same as his ultimate end for all of creation.

The Scriptures occasionally speak about the ultimate end of the *goodness* of the good part of the moral world. In other words, the Bible teaches what goal God has in mind for goodness (as found in his good moral agents). He wants this goodness to achieve certain purposes.

Certainly, we should hold strongly to the idea that whatever the ultimate end is of this goodness, it is the very thing that gives value to the moral world. It is the chief component that makes the moral world desirable, something that God himself wants. The virtue (or goodness) of a thing, after all, is in direct relationship with the ultimate end itself.

Thus we do well to believe that the ultimate end of this goodness is God's ultimate end for the entire moral world. He created the moral world as a place for this goodness to exist. Furthermore, once we combine this truth with Position 4, the ultimate end of this goodness is also God's ultimate end for the entire creation.

Again, the purpose of the goodness of a particular thing is the purpose of that thing as a whole, generally speaking. Remember, when someone makes something for a particular use, he labels that thing both good and valuable if it works well according to his design plan.

Position 10: God's ultimate end for his approved saints is the same as his ultimate end for all of creation.

The Bible describes certain persons as approved saints. These are people who are brought forward as highlights of true holy living. They are rightly considered, at least to some degree, to be included in the good part of the moral world that God created.

When we study their lives, we must ask what these approved saints sought after as their last and highest end in all they did. Since they were *approved* saints, we must suppose that what they sought was what they *ought* to have sought. Indeed, we discover from the Bible that they lived their lives in accordance with God's design plan for moral agents. We observe this reality in their holy conversation with God and in their approved and good behavior.

Taking this fact into account along with Position 9, whatever these approved saints sought after as their ultimate end is the very same thing God sought after as his ultimate end for creating the entire world.

Position 11: God's ultimate end for holy living is the same as his ultimate end for all of creation.

The Scripture teaches us that the good parts of the moral world are made up of people, both approved saints of the past and those who live in the present. Of those living in the present, let us consider the best among them when they are in their best state of being. This group of souls has a desire to aim their lives towards a particular goal or event. When they successfully do this, they will then exercise and express the goodness within them in a most natural and direct way. Likewise, they will express their respect to God in a proper and direct way.

I believe that the ultimate end desired by these pious souls is the ultimate end of holy living. It is the final destination point of the essential spirit of goodness. I also believe that the ultimate end of holy living is the exact same ultimate end God had in mind for the creation of the moral world. Do you see the logic in this connection? If so, then see the next logical step: If what these pious souls seek is the same as God's ultimate end in making the moral realm, then it is exactly the same as God's ultimate end for creating the entire world.

You see, it is without a doubt that the good and best part of the moral world will have a spirit of true goodness. This spirit of true goodness will lead them to have a natural desire and tendency to the ultimate end of goodness. When they arrive at the ultimate end of goodness, then they will also arrive at God's ultimate end for the moral world.

Furthermore, the best part of the moral world will also seek and desire the same end that God himself ultimately desires. They will want what he wants. His ultimate end for creating them and all other things will be the same ultimate end they seek after as they live out their lives. How could their desire to have true respect for God and friendship with him be expressed in any other way?

Position 12: The ultimate end sought by Jesus Christ
is the same as God's ultimate end for all of creation.

Our final interpretive position relates to the Lord Jesus Christ and the purpose he had in mind for living out his earthly life. Whatever Christ sought as his ultimate end must be exactly the same as God's ultimate end for creating the world as a whole.

How do we come to this conclusion? The Holy Scriptures teach us that Jesus Christ is the head of the moral world, especially the good part of it. Under Position 11, we discussed people who desire to live holy lives as servants of God. The Lord Jesus Christ is the chief of all God's servants! Indeed, he is the appointed head of all God's saints and angels. The Bible presents him as the highest and most perfect example of goodness. Thus when we take all the prior positions into account, it is clear that Christ's ultimate end for living his life is exactly the same as God's ultimate end for creating the world.

With this incredible fact, we bring a conclusion to Section II. Each of the twelve positions that have been expounded above will be extremely useful to us as we move forward into actual texts of Scripture. In the next several chapters, passage after passage will be presented and analyzed. I believe when we interpret these passages through the lens of the positions listed above, we will find them all in agreement with the conclusion of this work, namely, God made himself his own ultimate end when he created the world.

14
SCRIPTURE ON GOD'S GLORY AS HIS ULTIMATE END

We now begin Section III, looking directly to the Scriptures to teach us about the reason God made the world. Having established the twelve interpretive principles in the last chapter, we are ready to begin digging into various texts themselves, seeking answers as to what motivated the creative acts of God.

Section III: Scriptural demonstrations of God's Glory as his ultimate end in creating the world

Under Section I several general passages were mentioned that showed God's ultimate end in creation. We will be much more specific here, offering nine demonstrations from the Scriptures that God has himself as his end goal in all of his works and in his creation of the world as a whole.

Demonstration 1: Passages that present God's glory as the ultimate end of all his works

When we read God's words in Isaiah 48:11, we see that God makes himself his own end in his works. Everything he does, he does for his own sake. The verse further shows that the way in which he makes himself his own end in his works is by making *his glory* his ultimate end. The text reads as follows:

> **Isaiah 48:11** For my own sake, for my own sake, I do it, for how should my name be profaned? My glory I will not give to another.

Saying this is as much as saying, "I will obtain my end. I will not relinquish my glory. No other will take this prize from me."

It is pretty evident here that God's name and glory are spoken of in this text (his name and glory seem to mean the same thing, a point which will be examined later). The exaltation of his name and glory was his ultimate end for the great work detailed in the context.

Furthermore, God's glory is not referred to as an inferior or subordinate end. It is not the type of end that is merely subservient to the interests of other ends. This truth is expressed emphatically. The strong emphasis and repetition constrain us to understand that whatever God does is ultimately for his own sake – "For my own sake, even for my own sake I will do it."

In the same way, the words of the apostle Paul in Romans 11:36 lead us to the understanding that everything exists essentially for the purpose of bringing glory to God:

> **Romans 11:36** For from him and through him and to him are all things. To him be glory forever. Amen.

In the preceding context of this passage, the Apostle presents the marvelous ways of divine wisdom. Paul shows how all things that exist find their final issue and result in God. Just as they are from him at first and governed by him in their process, they also find their ultimate end in him.

As we study this section of Romans, Paul's discussion of this matter brings to light how God planned and brought all this to pass so that all things are "of," "through," and "to" him. His plan involved the setting up of the kingdom of Christ in the world, leaving the Jews, and calling the Gentiles. He also planned how he would later call in the Jews along with the fullness of the Gentiles. God's arrangement of these things included all the circumstances that went along with these wonderful works.

Surely it is evident to the reader that God is doing all of these things ultimately for his own glory! For example, in his plan and its outworking, God shows both his justice and goodness in very great ways. He, likewise, magnifies his grace and demonstrates the sovereignty and freeness of it. Indeed, the working of his glorious plan reveals the absolute dependence all people have on him.

Then, at the end of the passage (11:33-36), Paul breaks out into a deeply touching, rapturous exclamation. He expresses his great admiration of God's wisdom, so deep and divine. Paul is overwhelmed at the amazing process that God enacts in order to attain his end goal, causing all things to be "to him."

The final statement the Apostle makes is a glad and joyful consent to God's excellent design in all he does to glorify himself: "To him be glory forever!" Essentially, Paul is saying that since everything is so wonderfully orchestrated to work out for his glory, then let him have all this glory forevermore!

Demonstration 2: Passages that present God's glory as the ultimate end of the good part of the moral world

Remember, the good part of the moral world is made up of people (intelligent, moral beings) who actually love God and seek to obey him. Scripture clearly teaches that this segment of the moral realm exists expressly for the purpose of bringing glory to God. He is their ultimate end. For example, consider God's words in the following texts from the prophet Isaiah:

> **Isaiah 43:6-7** I will say to the north, Give up, and to the south, Do not withhold; bring my sons from afar and my daughters from the end of the earth, everyone who is called by my name, whom I created for my glory, whom I formed and made.

> **Isaiah 60:21** Your people shall all be righteous; they shall possess the land forever, the branch of my planting, the work of my hands, that I might be glorified.

> **Isaiah 61:3** . . . that they may be called oaks of righteousness, the planting of the LORD, that he may be glorified.

In each of these texts, the glory of God was the ultimate end, final aim, and main purpose of God's saints. God created them and gave them being for his own glory. Furthermore, he made them saints for the exact same purpose. As the text indicates, God had "made" and "formed" these people to be his sons and daughters, all for his own glory. They are the trees of righteousness that he had planted, the very work of his hands, so that ultimately he might be glorified through their lives.

When we read these verses carefully and study them closely, we must ask: Which was the ultimate end, God's glory or the happiness of his people? It would be very unnatural to interpret these texts as though God's glory were only an inferior or subordinate end to the happiness of his people. To see this we must carefully study the context of each passage. When we do, we discover that it is extremely strained and contextually unnatural to interpret these texts in such a way that makes the happiness of his people God's ultimate end.

Likewise, it would be unnatural to interpret these passages in such a way that implies God's glory was only part of the ultimate goal. This interpretation says that God was merely predicting that he would create, form, and plant his people – yes, so that he might be glorified in the process – but all ultimately for the end that God's people might be happy.

Both of the above readings seem erroneous when we interpret the passages properly in their contexts. These passages, when read naturally in their contextual flow, indicate that God does promise to make his people happy, *but it is so that ultimately he would be glorified in their joy,* not the other way around. (It is important to keep in mind here the difference between original, ultimate ends and consequential, ultimate ends, as discussed earlier in this work).

Taking in the whole context of Isaiah 43 clearly and plainly demonstrates the point I am making. Reading from the beginning of the chapter, it is clear that God was promising a future, great, and wonderful work of his power and grace. He promised to deliver his people from all their misery and make them exceedingly happy. But then he declared what end goal he had in mind for these works: It was all for his own glory. Indeed, being glorified was God's sum purpose for his design to save them. Here is the passage again with some of the surrounding context:

> **Isaiah 43:1-2; 4-7** I have redeemed you; I have called you by name, you are mine... When you walk through fire you shall not be burned, and the flame shall not consume you... you are precious in my eyes, and honored, I give men in return for you, peoples in exchange for your life. Fear not, for I am with you... I will... bring my sons from afar and my daughters from the end of the earth, everyone who is called by my name, whom I created for my glory.

The natural reading is clearly that God redeems, saves, and makes his people happy for the ultimate goal of bringing glory to his own name.

We notice this same reality when we look at the surrounding context of Isaiah 60:21. The entire chapter is made up totally of the promises God has made regarding the future. The essence of these promises relates to the exceeding happiness that will be brought to God's church. In order to be brief, we will consider only the two preceding verses:

> **Isaiah 60:19-20** The sun shall be no more your light by day, nor for brightness shall the moon give you light; but the LORD will be your everlasting light, and your God will be your glory. Your sun shall no more go down, nor your moon withdraw itself; for the LORD will be your everlasting light, and your days of mourning shall be ended.

Then in verse 21 we read, "Your people shall all be righteous; they shall possess the land forever, the branch of my planting, the work of my hands." Finally, after saying all this regarding the wonderful position and happiness of his people, God then adds his end goal in the process: "That I might be glorified."

All of the promises mentioned in these verses are a listing of the constituent parts of the exceeding happiness of God's people. But God's glory is mentioned as the end, final purpose, and the sum of God's design for the happiness of his people. It is not the other way around; namely, the happiness of God's people is not the ultimate end of the glory of God.

When we consider the promises of God in the context of Isaiah 61:3, it reveals the same truth:

> **Isaiah 61:3** To grant to those who mourn in Zion - to give them a beautiful headdress instead of ashes, the oil of gladness instead of mourning, the garment of praise instead of a faint spirit; that they may be called oaks of righteousness, the planting of the LORD, that he may be glorified.

Here, God promised that he would work to accomplish the joy, gladness, and happiness of his people, leading to the wonderful alleviation of mourning and sorrow. But the end goal of God's labor on behalf of his people is the bringing of glory to himself. Ultimately, his design plan and redeeming work lead to his glory and can be summed up as a God-glorifying process.

When we take these passages from Isaiah and interpret them in light of Position 7 (detailed earlier), then it is clear that the reason God created the world as a whole was for his own glory.

The same point can be argued from this text:

> **Jeremiah 13:11** For as the loincloth clings to the waist of a man, so I made the whole house of Israel and the whole house of Judah cling to me, declares the LORD, that they might be for me a people, a name, a praise, and a glory, but they would not listen.

This passage indicates that God was seeking to make Israel and Judah his own holy people. As the Apostle expresses it, God sought his peculiar people who were zealous for good works. Now, the reason God was seeking them in this way was so that they might be *a glory* to him.

In the days when Jeremiah was writing, the loincloth was used as a decorative ornament and as a badge of dignity and honor. So God desired his people to be a decorative ornament for his glory, a badge of dignity and honor (see verse 9 and also Is 3:24; 22:21; 23:10; Ex 28:8). When God speaks this way, it is unnatural to understand him as seeking merely a *subordinate* end. After all, he was seeking after a badge that he might wear it for his glory. He desired his peculiar and holy people to be that badge!

When human beings seek after a decorative ornament or badge for their garment, why do they do it? Are they seeking a badge for the sake of the badge? Of course not! They want it because when they wear it publicly, it brings them honor and glory.

It cannot be that God sought after his badge of glory merely for the good of others. It is unnatural to think that he had no regard for himself in his pursuit of his people. If that were true, the comparison Jeremiah makes to a badge of honor would make no sense. The following passages seem to be teaching this exact same doctrine:

> **Ephesians 1:5-6** He predestined us for adoption through Jesus Christ, according to the purpose of his will, to the praise of his glorious grace.
>
> **Isaiah 44:23** For the LORD has redeemed Jacob, and will be glorified in Israel.
>
> **Isaiah 49:3** You are my servant, Israel, in whom I will be glorified.
>
> **John 17:10** All mine are yours, and yours are mine, and I am glorified in them.
>
> **2 Thessalonians 1:10; 11-12** When he comes on that day to be glorified in his saints. . . To this end we always pray for you, that our God may make you worthy of his calling and may fulfill every resolve for good and every work of faith by his power, so that the name of our Lord Jesus may be glorified in you, and you in him, according to the grace of our God and the Lord Jesus Christ.

In the next chapter, we will continue with the third scriptural demonstration that God makes himself his own last end in creation.

15
CONCERNING THE MORAL PART OF CREATION

We now continue our analysis of various passages that demonstrate the reason God created the world, that it was ultimately for his own glory.

Demonstration 3: Passages that present God's glory as the ultimate end for the goodness of the moral part of creation

The Holy Scriptures occasionally indicate that God had a purpose in creating the *goodness* of the moral part of his creation. A survey of these passages confirms that he had himself in mind as the end for creating this goodness. The active goodness of certain individuals within the moral world was brought about by God ultimately to bring glory and honor to himself. Indeed, the reason their holy actions are considered to be virtuous and valuable is precisely because they bring glory to God. To show this from Scripture, consider this text:

> **Philippians 1:10-11** So that you may approve what is excellent, and so be pure and blameless for the day of Christ, filled with the fruit of righteousness that comes through Jesus Christ, to the glory and praise of God.

Here, the apostle Paul indicates that the fruits of righteousness which are visible in the lives of God's people are extremely valuable. After all, they fulfill the end he has planned for them, doing exactly what they are designed to do. According to the text, God designed his people to exist "through Jesus Christ" for "the glory and praise of God," and this is exactly how they live out their lives.

Jesus confirms this interpretation in John 15:8, "By this my Father is glorified, that you bear much fruit." Thus bringing glory to God is the great end of all true religious devotion and practice. The same truth is taught here:

> **1 Peter 4:11** Whoever speaks, as one who speaks oracles of God; whoever serves, as one who serves by the strength that God supplies - in order that in everything God may be glorified through Jesus Christ. To him belong glory and dominion forever and ever. Amen.

In this verse the apostle Peter directs Christians to regulate all their religious activities towards the one end of the glory of God.

Sometimes we find another variation of this theme in Scripture. In these cases the practicing of true religious devotion, repenting of sin, and turning towards holiness is expressed simply as the *glorifying* of God, as though this were the complete sum of the entire matter. The following passage is an example of this:

> **Revelation 11:13** Seven thousand people were killed in the earthquake, and the rest were terrified and gave glory to the God of heaven.

The same can be seen later in the same book:

> **Revelation 14:6-7** Then I saw another angel flying directly overhead, with an eternal gospel to proclaim to those who dwell on earth, to every nation and tribe and language and people. And he said with a loud voice, "Fear God and give him glory."

The phrase *give him glory* is written as though it is the total sum and ultimate end of all that is good and virtuous in religious practice and devotion. Furthermore, to *give him glory* is the ultimate end of the grand design of the preaching of the gospel throughout the entire world. To see this same point from the negative perspective, consider these words:

> **Revelation 16:9** They did not repent and give him glory.

This is just like saying that they did not leave their sins behind, and they did not turn in true faith to Christ. Thus God did not receive the great end he desires in the true religion he requires of men, namely, to be glorified. (Study these other passages which teach the same truth: Ps 22:21-23; Is 66:19; 24:15; 25:3; Jer 13:15-16; Dn 5:23; Rom 15:5-6).

Taking this thought a step further, when the Bible speaks of the influence of Christians upon others, it uses this same "glory" language. As already seen, when Christians exercise true devotion to the Lord and true virtue in their lives, the Bible indicates that they are *glorifying God.* Similarly, when true Christians influence other people, the goal is to lead them to glorify God as well. Here are two passages that support these ideas:

> **Matthew 5:16** In the same way, let your light shine before others, so that they may see your good works and give glory to your Father who is in heaven.

> **1 Peter 2:12** Keep your conduct among the Gentiles honorable, so that when they speak against you as evildoers, they may see your good deeds and glorify God on the day of visitation.

The apostle Paul provides another example. In Romans Paul raises a potential objection, or rather refers to one that others might raise. In doing so, he strongly suggests that the ultimate end of moral goodness or righteousness occurs when God's glory is attained.

> **Romans 3:7** But if through my lie God's truth abounds to his glory, why am I still being condemned as a sinner?

In other words (as the objection goes), if my sin leads to ultimate righteousness, which Paul describes as God's glory abounding, then why should my sin be grounds for my condemnation? Should I be punished for my sin if it has this result? Why shouldn't my vice be equivalent with my virtue if my vice results in God being glorified?

To further prove the point, some Scripture passages indicate that the glory of God is the ultimate end of certain actions of grace. The fact that these particular actions lead to God's glory is precisely why they are valuable actions. For example, consider the act of faith as it is described in the following verses:

> **Romans 4:20** No distrust made him waver concerning the promise of God, but he grew strong in his faith as he gave glory to God.

> **Philippians 2:11** And every tongue confess that Jesus Christ is Lord, to the glory of God the Father.

Or consider the act of repentance:

> **Joshua 7:19** My son, I beg you, give glory to the LORD God of Israel, and make confession to Him. (NKJV)

Next, the act of love:

> **2 Corinthians 8:19** We carry out this act of grace that is being ministered by us, for the glory of the Lord himself and to show our good will.

And also the acts of thanksgiving and praise:

> **Luke 17:18** Was no one found to return and give praise to God except this foreigner?

> **Psalm 50:23** The one who offers thanksgiving as his sacrifice glorifies me; to one who orders his way rightly I will show the salvation of God!

Concerning this last verse, it seems that God was speaking this to people who agreed that the end of all religion was to glorify God, but they thought this happened when their religious performances were at their highest. They believed God was glorified chiefly in the offering of a multitude of sacrifices. However, God corrected their mistake. He informed them that the grand end of religion is attained when the spiritual sacrifices of praise and holy conversation are offered. God is not glorified when people engage in mere outward religious activities.

All this data confirms that, according to the teaching of the Bible, God's glory is his ultimate end for the *goodness* of the moral part of his creation. One particular verse should be presented as a final support of this truth:

> **1 Corinthians 6:20** You are not your own, for you were bought with a price. So glorify God in your body [and in your spirit, which are his].

Here, giving glory to God is spoken of as the comprehensive summary of all religion. This includes Christ redeeming us and much more. The Apostle also urges us to understand that we do not belong to ourselves, and we should not act as though we do. We belong to God who alone has ownership over us. We should never use our bodies or the faculties of our souls for ourselves, but always for God, making him our end. Further, Paul expresses exactly how we are to make God our end, namely, by making his *glory* our end – "glorify God in your body [and in your spirit, which are his]."

In this verse it is impossible to pretend that God is merely a subordinate end. Christians should never seek God as an end that leads to another, more ultimate end, such as their own happiness. God is not subservient to their happiness. If they act chiefly and ultimately for the sake of their own selves, then they would be using themselves more as their own, rather than as God's. But that would directly contradict the design of Paul's exhortation and argument in this passage. He maintains that we should give ourselves away to God, using ourselves as his, since we are not our own. Every action ought to be for his sake and not for our own sakes.

When all of this evidence is taken together, it is clear that Position 9 is true. Indeed, his own glory is the ultimate end God desired when he created the world.

Demonstration 4: Passages that present God's requirement that people do everything to glorify him

In the previous section, we observed the reality that God created the actual goodness of the moral part of creation for his own glory. Now, we will look at this idea from a broader perspective, observing passages that require people to desire and seek after God's glory as their highest and ultimate end *in everything they do.* For example:

> **1 Corinthians 10:30-31** So, whether you eat or drink, or whatever you do, do all to the glory of God.
>
> **1 Peter 4:11** In order that in everything God may be glorified.

It can also be argued that those who follow Christ are required to seek the glory of God as their *primary ambition,* above every other thing in their lives.

We see this requirement of primacy in the prayer that Jesus gave to his disciples. He begins with the request, "Hallowed be thy name." Notice carefully that this desire stands first in Christ's prayer; it is primary. Furthermore, this petition forms a pattern and rule that his followers are to live by.

As we study this prayer, we should ask: What does this petition really mean? If it stands first and primary, every follower of Christ should labor to understand it. Quite simply in the language of the Bible, *hallowed be thy name* means the same as *glorified be your name* (this is clear from Lv

10:3, Ez 28:22, and from many other places). Thus Jesus petitions the Father first and foremost with the request that God's name be glorified.

Now, it's obvious that our ultimate and highest end should be the primary thing we desire. There should be nothing we want more than the glory of God. Additionally, whatever is first in our desires should also be first in our prayers. So we could argue this way: Since Christ directs us to put God's glory first in our prayers, therefore, God's glory is our ultimate end.

This truth is further confirmed when we consider the conclusion of the Lord's Prayer: "For yours is the kingdom, the power, and the glory." This conclusion is organically connected to every other petition in the prayer. In other words, all the other requests must be made under the auspices of the dominion and glory of God. Everything we desire of the Lord and ask for in our prayers must ultimately be for the sake of God's dominion and glory. The followers of Christ should not pray with any other end goal in mind.

Notice that God's glory and dominion are the first two things mentioned in the prayer (indeed, they are the subject of the first half of the prayer). They are also the final two things mentioned in the conclusion. This means that God's glory is the Alpha and Omega of the prayer.

From all these facts we may argue, in accordance with Position 8, that God's glory is the last end of creation.

Demonstration 5: Passages that present God's glory as the ultimate end for what delights the best part of the moral world

In addition to the broad requirements for people to glorify God in all they do, there are some texts that focus on what it is that delights the heart of God's people. These texts also indicate that God's glory is an ultimate end of creation.

In order to see it, we must examine the earnest desires of the best part of the moral world. We must analyze their hearts and see what delights them most. Furthermore, we must observe them while they are in their very best frames of thinking.

Remember, these are the people who naturally tend to have a spirit of true goodness. They are deeply interested in conforming their lives to match God's design plan for them when he created them.

As we look carefully at these lives, we see that the virtuous and pious affections of their hearts seem to be set on the glory of God. The glory of God is the object which attracts and delights them more than anything else. The glory of God is what they want, and it is what they are designed to want.

For example, consider how the holy apostles often spoke of their high regard for God, the Supreme One. It's obvious they were exercising true and deep devotion to the Lord as they breathed out these praises to him:

Romans 11:36 To him be glory forever. Amen.

Romans 16:27 To the only wise God be glory forevermore through Jesus Christ! Amen.

Galatians 1:4-5 [Christ] gave himself for our sins to deliver us from the present evil age, according to the will of our God and Father, to whom be the glory forever and ever. Amen.

2 Timothy 4:18 The Lord will rescue me from every evil deed and bring me safely into his heavenly kingdom. To him be the glory forever and ever. Amen.

Ephesians 3:21 To him be glory in the church and in Christ Jesus throughout all generations, forever and ever. Amen.

Hebrews 13:21 Through Jesus Christ, to whom be glory forever and ever. Amen.

Philippians 4:20 To our God and Father be glory forever and ever. Amen.

2 Peter 3:18 To him be the glory both now and to the day of eternity. Amen.

> **Jude 1:25** To the only God, our Savior, through Jesus Christ our Lord, be glory, majesty, dominion, and authority, before all time and now and forever. Amen.

> **Revelation 1:5-6** To him who loves us. . . to him be glory and dominion forever and ever. Amen.

We see similar affection for the glory of God in the heart of the holy king David. As the sweet psalmist of Israel, David poured out the deep, genuine desires of his heart, giving God the honor he deserves. Here is an example of David's pious heart overflowing in this way:

> **1 Chronicles 16:28-29** Ascribe to the LORD, O clans of the peoples, ascribe to the LORD glory and strength! Ascribe to the LORD the glory due his name. (See also Ps 29:1-2; 57:5; 72:18-19; 96:7-8; 115:1)

These same types of expressions are meant to flow from the hearts of the whole church as well. When we study Isaiah 42:10-12, we see all of God's people giving him praise and honor throughout every part of the earth.

In the same way, the saints and angels who are now in heaven have the same desires. They join their hearts and voices in the chorus of praise, expressing deep and sincere devotion for God. In Revelation 4:9 this love for the Lord's glory springs powerfully and naturally from their hearts (see also 4:11-14; 7:12).

Likewise, in a wonderful vision, Isaiah saw the seraphim engaged in this same heavenly worship. Notice how they especially exulted in their praise of God's glory:

> **Isaiah 6:2-3** Above him stood the seraphim. . . And one called to another and said: "Holy, holy, holy is the LORD of hosts; the whole earth is full of his glory!"

When Jesus was born, they also worshipped him in this same way:

> **Luke 2:14** Glory to God in the highest, and on earth peace among those with whom he is pleased!

It is obvious that these holy inhabitants of earth and heaven do not consider the glory of God to be a mere subordinate end. As we read of their desire, it is clear that in their view God's glory has innate value to the *highest degree*. It would be absurd to say that their highest interest was benevolence to their fellow creatures. This would, indeed, be a poor interpretation of their ardent exclamations.

Furthermore, it would be absurd to say that they are only interested in the glory of God because it is a means to the further end of the happiness of God's people. God's glory is not a means to *any* other end. It would be terribly erroneous to interpret their expressions in that way. Their earnest desires are for the glory of God as the ultimate end of all. They are not speaking of their love for themselves or for their fellow creatures. Rather, they are expressing their exalted and supreme regard to the Most High, the only infinitely glorious being, almighty God.

Consider another passage of Scripture: "Not to us, O LORD, not to us, but to your name give glory" (Psalm 115:1). Here the church is expressing her deepest desire. It would be absurd to say that she only desires to give God glory as a necessary or convenient means to her own advancement and pleasure. God's glory alone is the ultimate goal of her expressed desire.

From all the facts discovered in these passages, it is clear by Position 11 that God's glory is the ultimate end of creation.

In the next chapter, we will continue our list of scriptural demonstrations, shifting our analysis to passages that speak of the Lord Jesus Christ. Why did he come into the world? What was his purpose in life and death? What was his ultimate end for bringing about the redemption of God's people? By this point in our study, it is doubtful that you will be surprised by the answer the Bible gives to these questions.

16
Redemption in Jesus for the Glory of God

We will now consider the sixth and seventh scriptural demonstrations. Both of these show that God made himself his ultimate end and highest goal for creating the world. Among all the demonstrations, these two are extremely important because they focus on Christ's work on the cross to save guilty sinners.

Demonstration 6: Passages that present God's glory as the ultimate end sought by Jesus Christ

The glory of God was the ultimate and highest end Christ sought in his life, as his words in this passage indicate:

> **John 7:18** The one who speaks on his own authority seeks his own glory, but the one who seeks the glory of him who sent him is true, and in him there is no falsehood.

Jesus was effectively stating that he had not come to earth merely seeking "his own glory." Don't misunderstand him. It wouldn't be reasonable to conclude that he had no regard *at all* for his own glory. This is true even if he only meant no glory as far as his human nature was concerned. After all, part of the reward promised to him was glory in that very human nature. It was for this glory that "the joy was set before him" as he endured the cross. Thus he did not mean that his own glory was unimportant, but rather that it was not his *ultimate* aim. Which is to say that it was not the final end governing all his conduct.

In the latter part of John 7:18, Christ informs us exactly what he was seeking as a higher goal than his own glory: "The one who seeks the glory of him who sent him is true." Indeed, it was the Father's glory that Christ sought as his ultimate aim. He did not intend to minimize his own glory, but he was showing that the Father's glory was his supreme governing end.

> **John 12:27-28** Now is my soul troubled. And what shall I say? "Father, save me from this hour"? But for this purpose I have come to this hour. Father, glorify your name.

The context of this passage describes Jesus' journey to Jerusalem, where he expected to be crucified within a few days. As he drew near, the prospect of his last sufferings was extremely terrible to him. Under this heavy distress of mind, Jesus provided support for himself by considering what the outcome of his sufferings would bring, namely, great glory to God.

When an acting agent decides to engage in a difficult work, he needs help to succeed in it. If the end of the work is a wonderful end, he can find help by reminding himself of it. When he remembers that the goal, when achieved, will be simply amazing, he finds strength and support to face the difficulties of the work and not to give up.

Furthermore, above the other ends, his *ultimate* and *supreme* end functions this way. This is because his ultimate and supreme end is more valuable than the others, and it can provide a counteracting effect to the difficult means which lead to that end. Thus by remembering his ultimate end, he finds rest and support in his hard work. When this ultimate end is brought to mind, he is encouraged to keep going toward the goal. After all, this end is, in itself, agreeable and sweet to him, and it is this end that ultimately fulfills his desire. It is the central source of comfort for him in carrying out his difficult work. It is what delights his heart, providing great joy for him, even though his journey to the goal will be excruciating.

In this passage as stated above, the soul of Jesus Christ was hurting and distressed as he considered the most difficult part of his work (difficult by an infinite degree). The time for this painful work was at hand, the cross was looming inevitably in his near future. In the midst of this conflict and anguish, his mind was seeking comfort and support by considering the final goal of his incredibly difficult work.

Now certainly, if his mind was seeking comfort by reflecting on the end goal, then his mind would most naturally consider the *highest* end of the work, since this would have provided the strongest support for him. After all, his soul was deeply troubled and in anguish. He was anticipating a task that would be utterly painful and difficult. He desperately needed support and comfort.

As he pondered the highest end of his work, we see that he immediately thought of the glory of God, his Father. In this precious thought – that God would be glorified in his excruciating journey – Jesus found comfort and encouragement. The glory of God was the end goal that pleased and supported his soul most, and it was why he was willing to lay down his life.

Here is another passage where we see the same thing, Christ seeking the glory of God as his ultimate end. He was drawing even nearer to his last sufferings on the cross, spending time with his disciples, praying with them for the final time on the evening before he was crucified. In this remarkable prayer, Jesus expressed the sum total of his aims and desires in his upcoming work:

> **John 17:1** Father, the hour has come; glorify your Son that the Son may glorify you.

Notice, these were Christ's first words in the prayer. As his initial request, we may consider it to be his supreme request, expressing what he most desired. In other words, this was what he was ultimately aiming at in all his upcoming sufferings. When we consider the rest of the prayer, all the way to its conclusion, we find it all to be an amplification of this one great request, that the Son may glorify the Father.

When all the textual evidence is considered, it is substantially clear that Jesus sought the glory of God as his highest and last end. Thus by Position 12, this was God's last end in the creation of the world.

Demonstration 7: Passages that present redemption as being for the glory of God

This is clear from Scripture: The last end of the greatest work of God's providence (the work of redemption in Jesus Christ) is the glory of God. The clarity of this truth can be observed in the previous point, where we saw that the ultimate end sought by Jesus Christ, the Redeemer, was the glory of God.

Furthermore, this point becomes even clearer if we study the contexts of the passages mentioned above. Each of those passages operate in isolation as proof of Christ's last end in his great work to acquire redemption for his people. But when we dig deeper into the surrounding contexts, we see the same truth to an even greater degree.

As we noted above from John 7:18, Christ did not seek his own glory in what he did, rather he sought the glory of the one who sent him. Contextually, we see that he was referring specifically to his work of redemption, the primary work of ministry he came into the world to perform.

In the next text above, John 12:27-28, Christ was comforting himself as he considered the extremely difficult work which lay ahead of him. The comfort he found came from his understanding of the highest, ultimate, and most excellent end of his work. This work was what his heart was most set upon and what his heart most delighted in.

As we consider the deeper context of this passage, we see that the Father gave Christ an answer from heaven at exactly the time when Jesus needed comfort. This answer comes in the latter part of verse 28, where the Father said, "I have glorified it, and I will glorify it again."

The meaning of this response from the Father is plain. God had glorified his name in what Christ had already done up to that point in his ministry. The Father had sent him to do a work, and as Christ had carried out this work, the Father received glory. Furthermore, the Father said he would glorify his name *again* and to a greater degree in what Christ would do next. There would be even greater glory for the Father when Christ succeeded in the work of redemption.

Jesus demonstrated that he understood all this in what he said next. After the people around had heard the voice of the Father from heaven (some said it was thunder while others thought it might be an angel), Christ said to them, "This voice has come for your sake, not mine."

After saying this Jesus made another statement, revealing his exceedingly great joy in the prospect of bringing glory to God. He desired to bring God the highest glory by successfully accomplishing the work of redemption, even though it meant great suffering. He said:

> **John 12:31-32** Now is the judgment of this world; now will the ruler of this world be cast out. And I, when I am lifted up from the earth, will draw all people to myself.

As we observed before, Jesus placed his own glory in the success of the work of redemption:

> **John 12:23-24** The hour has come for the Son of Man to be glorified. Truly, truly, I say to you, unless a grain of wheat falls into the earth and dies, it remains alone; but if it dies, it bears much fruit.

From these verses it is clear that Jesus was seeking both his own and the Father's glory in the prayer of John 17. He sought after this glory as the end of the great work he had come into the world to do, which he would soon finish. When we look at the context of the whole prayer, these facts are made plain. This is particularly true of verses 4 and 5:

> **John 17:4-5** I glorified you on earth, having accomplished the work that you gave me to do. And now, Father, glorify me in your own presence.

This passage makes the doctrine fairly simple to understand. Jesus declared to his Father that he had successfully glorified him here on the earth. He had completed the redemptive work which his Father had given him.

This monumental task had been given to him by God for a *particular end,* that God might be *glorified.*

So Jesus had come into the world to lay the foundation for the glory of God and had now finished laying it. This foundation provided the way for the Father to obtain his will. Christ's self-denying work provided the means for the Father to bring about the highest peaks of what he had designed. It is abundantly clear that the highest peak of God's design was his own glory, John 17:4-5 showing that God's glory is his *ultimate end* in the great work of redemption.

Another example is found in John 13:31-32. This text indicates that while bringing about the plan of redemption, Christ was encouraged and delighted in God's glory as he suffered. It was the glory of the Father (and indeed, his own glory with the Father) that was his highest end and that gave Christ the motivation to move forward into his approaching sufferings.

In this passage Judas had gone out to betray Jesus. In this foreboding situation, Christ had his heart set mainly on the glory of God as his supreme delight. He made it plain that the glory of God was the ultimate end for which he was willing to suffer:

> **John 13:31-32** When [Judas] had gone out, Jesus said, "Now is the Son of Man glorified, and God is glorified in him. If God is glorified in him, God will also glorify him in himself, and glorify him at once."

As you can see, the doctrine is very obvious in this passage. Likewise, when Christ was born, confirmation of the doctrine can be heard in the song of the angels:

> **Luke 2:14** Glory to God in the highest, and on earth peace among those with whom he is pleased!

Surely we are correct in thinking that these singing angels knew what they were singing about. They understood what God's last end was for sending Christ into the world. On this occasion they were rejoicing in the coming of Christ. No doubt, their minds would have rejoiced mostly in what was *most valuable and glorious* in the sending and coming of Christ, and this very thing would be the chief and ultimate end of the mission he was coming to achieve.

Furthermore, we do well to believe these singing angels would have fixated their minds so intently on this ultimate and glorious end that it would be the first thing they sung about. The song, after all, was a way for them to express the sentiments of their minds and the exultations of their hearts.

Another place where the glory of the Father and Son is spoken of as the end of the work of redemption is Philippians 2:6-11. Here, we find language very similar to what we saw in John 12:23, 28; 13:31-32; 17:1-5.

> **Philippians 2:6-11** Who, though he was in the form of God, did not count equality with God a thing to be grasped, but made himself nothing, taking the form of a servant, being born in the likeness of men. And being found in human form, he humbled himself by becoming obedient to the point of death, even death on a cross. Therefore God has highly exalted him and bestowed on him the name that is above every name, so that at the name of Jesus every knee should bow. . . and every tongue confess that Jesus Christ is Lord, to the glory of God the Father.

We find the same truth in Ephesians 1, where the praise of God's glory is referred to as the end of the work of redemption:

> **Ephesians 1:3-6** Blessed be the God and Father of our Lord Jesus Christ, who has blessed us in Christ with every spiritual blessing in the heavenly places, even as he chose us in him. . . he predestined us for adoption. . . to the praise of his glorious grace.

As this passage continues, the same truth is mentioned again. That is, when it comes to the redemption of Christ, God's glory is the great end of it all, as verse 12 reiterates.

Prior to verse 12, several things are mentioned that belong to God's great redemption. Included are God's great wisdom in redemption (v.8), the clearness of the light that comes through Christ (v.9), and the gathering together by God of all things into one, things in heaven and things on earth, all in Christ (v.10). Then we read of God's granting an interest in this great redemption to those first converted to Christian faith from among the Jews (v.11). After these thoughts are articulated, then follows the great end of God's work of redemption:

> **Ephesians 1:12** So that we who were the first to hope in Christ might be to the praise of his glory.

After this statement we read that the same great salvation is also bestowed upon the Gentiles. First, the beginning of this bestowment is mentioned as its first fruits grow in *this* world. Then in the next two verses, we read of the completion of this process in *another* world.

> **Ephesians 1:13-14** In him you also, when you heard the word of truth, the gospel of your salvation, and believed in him, were sealed with the promised Holy Spirit, who is the guarantee of our inheritance until we acquire possession of it, to the praise of his glory.

We find these same truths expressed in a similar way here:

> **2 Corinthians 4:14-15** He who raised the Lord Jesus will raise us also with Jesus and bring us with you into his presence. For it is all for your sake, so that as grace extends to more and more people it may increase thanksgiving, to the glory of God.

When we look into the Old Testament, we find the end of the great work of redemption spoken of in the same way:

> **Psalm 79:9** Help us, O God of our salvation, for the glory of your name; deliver us, and atone for our sins, for your name's sake!

We see it again when we read of the Old Testament prophecies concerning Jesus Christ:

> **Isaiah 44:23** Sing, O heavens, for the LORD has done it; shout, O depths of the earth; break forth into singing, O mountains, O forest, and every tree in it! For the LORD has redeemed Jacob, and will be glorified in Israel.

In these words we see that created objects are called upon to rejoice at the attainment of God's glory in the redemption of his people. This is the exact same end that the angels rejoiced in when Jesus was born (see Is 48:10-11; 49:3).

From these examples it is clear that the glory of God is the ultimate end of the work of redemption. And redemption is God's chief work of providence towards the moral world. The Scriptures are abundantly clear on these points, and they become even clearer when we understand that the whole universe is subject to Jesus Christ. All of heaven and earth, all angels and men, are subject to Christ who carries out his kingly office. All of these things are put under him for a purpose, that he might order them in such a way that they serve the great designs of the plan of redemption.

He says of himself that all power is given to him. All the power of heaven and all the power of earth are his. He possesses this universal authority so that he may give eternal life to every person the Father has given to him.

He is exalted far above all principality and power and over all might and dominion. He is made head over all things for the good of the church. The angels are also put into subjection beneath him, and he employs them as ministering spirits to bring good to them who are the heirs of salvation.

The Redeemer governs all things in this way so that the recipients of his great salvation receive all of his benefits. This is true of things that are presently here and of things to come.

Additionally, God's works of providence in and through the moral governments of the world are also evidently subordinate to the great purposes of the wondrous work of redemption. When we read accounts of these governments in the historical texts of Scripture or when we read what was foretold of them in the prophetic portions, we always see them subordinate to God's great end in the process – his own glory.

Besides all this, it is the work of redemption that makes people good to begin with, so that they will glorify God with their lives. After all, redemption is the process where people are restored to holiness and happiness in God's sight. The Bible speaks of the work of redemption as becoming a new creation, where people are brought into a new existence or made into new creatures.

From all these truths it follows, in accordance to Positions 5, 6, and 7, that the glory of God is the ultimate end of the creation of the world.

There are two more scriptural demonstrations left for us to consider. These will be the focus of the next chapter.

17
JUDGMENT DAY AND ALL WORKS OF PROVIDENCE

The final two demonstrations from Scripture will now be analyzed. These reveal (as do the demonstrations covered in previously) that the Bible clearly teaches God makes himself his own ultimate end in the creation of the world.

Demonstration 8: Passages that present all moral goodness as being for the glory of God

The Bible leads us to believe that bringing glory to himself is God's last end in his *moral government* of the world, generally speaking. We have already seen this truth revealed in some of its varied aspects. Certainly, we have seen this to be particularly true in relation to God's work of redemption, which is chief among all his administrative works as he governs the moral world.

I have also indicated that God requires the subjects of his moral government to seek his glory as their last end. As a requirement of God, it is their duty to seek it. Seeking his glory is, indeed, the last end of all the moral goodness that God requires of them. Furthermore, God's glory is the highest and most significant part of all their moral goodness, and so it is the most valuable aspect of it. Also, this is the chief end that Jesus Christ sought in his earthly life, and he is the person whom God has set as the head and chief governor of this moral world.

It has also been shown that God made certain parts of the moral world good. That is, they exist in order to be good and seek goodness. We have seen that when they exist for the good and seek after the good, it is the glory of God that is their chief end.

Now, I would like to look further at what the Bible has to say about God's establishment of *public worship* and his *ordinances* among human beings. It will be shown that the end of these establishments is the same end we have seen over and over again, namely, the glory of God. First, observe the words of God spoken through the prophet Haggai regarding public worship:

> **Haggai 1:8** Go up to the hills and bring wood and build the house, that I may take pleasure in it and that I may be glorified, says the LORD.

The glory of God is also spoken of as the end and purpose of God's promises of rewards and his fulfillment of prophecies:

> **2 Corinthians 1:20** For all the promises of God find their Yes in him. That is why it is through him that we utter our Amen to God for his glory.

Further, the glory of God is spoken of as the end and purpose of God's continued threats to punish sin:

> **Numbers 14:20-22** Then the LORD said, "I have pardoned, according to your word. But truly, as I live, and as all the earth shall be filled with the glory of the LORD."

When this passage is carefully studied, it becomes clear that the glory of Jehovah ("LORD" in English) is God's highest and ultimate end. So it is the thing he cannot and will not fail to bring about. It is most important to him everywhere and in every case throughout every part of his dominion. This is true regardless of what becomes of man.

This means that God's glory will not be compromised, even in his compassion on sinners. Whatever abatements he might make regarding the judgments that people deserve, it will not be the kind of lessening or changing of judgment that compromises his glory. Under no circumstances will the attainment of God's glory as his chief and highest end be placed second to some other goal he might have, not even his compassion on sinners. This is why the glory of God is spoken of in the Bible as the highest end of God's executing judgments on his enemies in the world. Consider a few more passages that teach this truth:

> **Exodus 14:17-18** And I will get glory over Pharaoh and all his host. . .

> **Ezekiel 28:22** Thus says the Lord GOD: "Behold, I am against you, O Sidon, and I will manifest my glory in your midst. And they shall know that I am the LORD when I execute judgments in her and manifest my holiness in her."

The next passage is along the same lines in the same book:

> **Ezekiel 39:13** All the people of the land will bury them, and it will bring them renown on the day that I show my glory, declares the Lord GOD.

So it is plain that the glory of God is the highest and ultimate end of the executions of his wrath. But this same end is also what God has in mind when he exercises his glorious mercy. And it is the same end he has in mind in both the misery and happiness that will be known in another world, as seen here:

> **Romans 9:22-23** What if God, desiring to show his wrath and to make known his power, has endured with much patience vessels of wrath prepared for destruction, in order to make known the riches of his glory for vessels of mercy, which he has prepared beforehand for glory.

Additionally, the glory of God is spoken of as the end purpose of the Day of Judgment. This is the time appointed by God to exercise his highest authority as the moral governor of the world. It is, as it were, the day of the consummation of God's moral government as it pertains to all his subjects in heaven, earth, and hell:

> **2 Thessalonians 1:9-10** They will suffer the punishment of eternal destruction, away from the presence of the Lord and from the glory of his might, when he comes on that day to be glorified in his saints, and to be marveled at among all who have believed.

On that day God's glory will be obtained among both saints and sinners. So from all these things it is plainly clear by Position 4 that God's glory is the ultimate end of the creation of the world.

Demonstration 9: Passages that present God's general works of providence as being for his God

From what has already been discussed, it certainly appears from Scripture that the glory of God is the last end of all his many and varied works. And conversely, it also shows that his glory is what most certainly results from his works of providence and from his having created the world. Putting all of this together in broad and general terms, God's glory is the highest good attained by any of his works, and his glory is the resulting consequence of all his creative and providential works.

In other words, not only do we find in Scripture specific instances where God seeks his own glory, but we also find broad and general language indicating that all of God's works of providence, when taken together as a set, are performed for the same purpose.

Psalm 8, for example, is a place where all the works of creation are celebrated. The psalmist mentions the heavens, the work of God's fingers, and the moon and stars, which he ordained to exist. He further refers to human beings as having been created a little lower than the angels. Other created objects are mentioned as well. Here is how it starts:

> **Psalm 8:1** O LORD, our Lord, how majestic is your name in all the earth! You have set your glory above the heavens.

The phrase "above the heavens" could be understood as *sitting upon the heavens*. That is, as high as the heavens are God's glory is higher than they. The words "name" and "glory" mean very much the same thing in this verse, as they do in many other places. We will see some more particular examples of this below.

We also find that Psalm 8 concludes in the same way it begins:

> **Psalm 8:9** O LORD, our Lord, how majestic is your name in all the earth!

We find a similar example of accounting all of God's creative and providential works to the ultimate end of his glory in Psalm 148. Here, the psalmist provides a list of most of the particular works of creation, enumerating them in order. Finally he declares:

> **Psalm 148:13** Let them praise the name of the LORD, for his name alone is exalted; his majesty is above earth and heaven.

Again, we see this same pattern in Psalm 104, where an even more particular and magnificent list of God's many works in creation and common providence is presented. In connection with this great list, we read:

> **Psalm 104:31** May the glory of the LORD endure forever; may the LORD rejoice in his works.

Notice that God's glory is spoken of as the *grand result* and *blessed consequence* of his works. This is precisely why he rejoices in them. When we read the song of the seraphim from the book of Isaiah, this same truth is doubtlessly implied in the lyrics of their song:

> **Isaiah 6:3** Holy, holy, holy is the LORD of hosts; the whole earth is full of his glory!

So the glory of God is both the joyful result and happy consequence of all his works of providence, generally speaking. This being the case, we are correct to further infer that the glory of God is also the consequence and result of all of creation.

To explain, when something is made for a particular use, and it is used in that way to obtain a good, then the good obtained is the happy consequence and result of having made the thing. For example, when a watchmaker constructs a watch, the good goal of its construction is obtained when someone actually determines the time of day from it. Likewise, being able to determine the time of day is the good consequence of making the watch. It is the same with God's creation. The glory of God is the actual result and consequence of his creating the world. As we have already noted, this appears to be what God seeks that is good, valuable, and excellent in itself.

By the way, nobody should pretend there is something that would render the glory of God valuable in some instances where it is obtained but worthless in others. If God's glory is desirable as an effect of all his works as a set, it will also be desirable as an effect of each and every individual work he performs, not just some of them. God never performs a work where his glory obtains, but it is not a desirable consequence of the work. So when his glory is obtained by creating the world, this is the most desirable and valued effect of his work. Therefore, it is plainly clear by Position 3 that the glory of God is the ultimate end of the creation of the world.

This brings us to the end of Section III and the nine biblical demonstrations. Each of these shows that God makes himself his own last end in creation. Again, this means that his primary goal in bringing things into existence was to glorify himself.

Next, we begin Section IV, where a summary of God's purposes for creating the world will be given. When we take all the biblical data together, three major purposes come to the surface related to why God created the world.

18
FOR THE SAKE OF HIS NAME

In Section III we carefully discussed nine major demonstrations from the Bible that support the truth proposed in this work, namely, that God created the world ultimately for his own glory. We now begin to unpack Section IV, taking what we have learned in the previous sections and building a summary from it. When we take all the biblical data together, and interpret it correctly in light of the positions detailed earlier, we find that God had three major purposes for creating the world:

Section IV: For the sake of his name, so that his perfections will be known, and so that he will be praised

In the next three chapters, we will take time to analyze each of these purposes, showing the scriptural support for them. We begin with the first purpose:

    A. For the sake of his name

Here, I will first bring to notice several passages that speak of God's name. These passages will show that his name is the object he most highly regards and is most concerned about. Those who are his virtuous, holy, and intelligent creatures all focus on his name in this same way.

We will also notice that the name of God is spoken of in Scripture much the same way as *God's glory* is. For example, God's name is spoken of as the end of his acts of goodness towards the good part of the moral world. Likewise, God's name is referred to as the end of his works of mercy and salvation towards his people. This is the same as it is with the glory of God, which is also spoken of as the end of these things. Consider these passages:

> **1 Samuel 12:22** For the LORD will not forsake his people, for his great name's sake.
>
> **Psalm 23:3** He restores my soul. He leads me in paths of righteousness for his name's sake.
>
> **Psalm 31:3** For your name's sake you lead me and guide me.
>
> **Psalm 109:21** But you. . . deal on my behalf for your name's sake.

In particular we often read in Scripture of the forgiveness of sins being for the sake of God's name:

> **1 John 2:12** I am writing to you, little children, because your sins are forgiven for his name's sake.
>
> **Psalm 25:11** For your name's sake, O LORD, pardon my guilt, for it is great.
>
> **Psalm 79:9** Help us, O God of our salvation, for the glory of your name; deliver us, and atone for our sins, for your name's sake!
>
> **Jeremiah 14:7** Though our iniquities testify against us, act, O LORD, for your name's sake.

These verses show that the salvation provided by Christ is for the sake of God's name. So when he leads and guides his people in the way of safety and happiness, restoring their souls and forgiving their sins, he is doing it for the *sake of his own name*. When he provides help, deliverance, and saving grace, which are all part of the grand salvation he extends, he is doing it all for the *sake of his own name*.

Consider two temporal salvations of God's people, the redemption from Egypt and the redemption from Babylon. These two salvation events are often represented as being prefigures of the redemption Christ brings to his people. They are temporal patterns of God's redemptive work in Jesus, pointing to him. They show us the basic process of redemption and how God brings it about.

When we study these two salvation events, we find they are frequently referred to as being brought forth for the *sake of God's name*. Notice this in the following passages, which are focused on God's deliverance of his people from Egypt and his bringing them into the land of Canaan:

> **2 Samuel 7:23** And who is like your people Israel, the one nation on earth whom God went to redeem to be his people, making himself a name. . .
>
> **Psalm 106:8** Yet he saved them for his name's sake. . .
>
> **Isaiah 63:12** [God] caused his glorious arm to go at the right hand of Moses, who divided the waters before them to make for himself an everlasting name.

Likewise, in Ezekiel 20 God relists various parts of his wondrous work of deliverance. As he gives this rehearsal, he adds the following in various places throughout the text:

> **Ezekiel 20:9** I acted for the sake of my name, that it should not be profaned in the sight of the nations. . . (See also Ez 20:14, 22; Jo 7:8-9; Dn 9:15)

We see much the same language in regard to God's redemption of his people from the Babylonian captivity:

> **Isaiah 48:9, 11** For my name's sake I defer my anger. . . For my own sake, for my own sake, I do it, for how should my name be profaned?

In Ezekiel the vindication of God's name is given as the reason he shows mercy and brings restoration to Israel:

> **Ezekiel 36:21-23** But I had concern for my holy name. . . Thus says the Lord GOD: It is not for your sake, O house of Israel, that I am about to act, but for the sake of my holy name. . . And I will vindicate the holiness of my great name, which has been profaned among the nations.

The same truth is confirmed here:

> **Ezekiel 39:25** Therefore thus says the Lord GOD: Now I will restore the fortunes of Jacob and have mercy on the whole house of Israel, and I will be jealous for my holy name.

This same truth is also confirmed in the book of Daniel, when Daniel prayed that God would forgive his people and show them mercy for *God's own sake* (see Dn 9:19). Indeed, these kinds of texts are found from time to time throughout Scripture, where God speaks of showing mercy, exercising goodness, and promoting his people's happiness *for his name's sake*.

When God speaks this way, we must understand what he means. He does not mean that his name is merely a subordinate end. It would be absurd to say that God promoted the happiness of his people for the sake of his name, but in subordination to their good! Or to say that his name is only exalted for the sake of his people as a means of promoting their happiness! How can that be possible? It can't! Especially when this type of language is used: "For my own sake, for my own sake, I do it, for how should my name be profaned?" And "It is not for your sake...but for the sake of my holy name."

Again, these texts represent the truth that God's people have their existence (at least their existence as God's people) for the sake of God's name. This is strongly implied when the text plainly indicates that God redeems or purchases people *for his name*. This is true in a passage that was mentioned earlier:

> **2 Samuel 7:23** Your people Israel, the one nation on earth whom God went to redeem to be his people, making himself a name...

Similarly:

> **Jeremiah 13:11** For as the loincloth clings to the waist of a man, so I made the whole house of Israel... cling to me... that they might be for me a people, a name...

And in the book of Acts:

> **Acts 15:14** Simeon has related how God first visited the Gentiles, to take from them a people for his name.

The truth that God redeems people for the sake of his name is also spoken of in Scripture as the end and purpose of the virtue, religious devotion, and holy behavior of God's saints. Study these texts to see this:

> **Romans 1:5** Through whom we have received grace and apostleship to bring about the obedience of faith for the sake of his name among all the nations.

> **Matthew 19:29** Everyone who has left houses or brothers... for my name's sake, will receive a hundredfold and will inherit eternal life.

> **3 John 1:7** For they have gone out for the sake of the name, accepting nothing from the Gentiles.

> **Revelation 2:3** You are enduring patiently and bearing up for my name's sake, and you have not grown weary.

Furthermore, we find God's holy people expressing their desire for and joy in God's name, just as they desire and find joy in God's glory:

> **2 Samuel 7:26** And your name will be magnified forever. . .

> **Psalm 76:1** In Judah God is known; his name is great in Israel.

> **Psalm 148:13** Let them praise the name of the LORD, for his name alone is exalted; his majesty is above earth and heaven.

"Majesty" has the same meaning in that verse as the term "glory." Two more examples:

> **Psalm 135:13** Your name, O LORD, endures forever, your renown, O LORD, throughout all ages.

> **Isaiah 12:4** Make known his deeds among the peoples, proclaim that his name is exalted.

Similarly, the Bible often speaks of the various judgments of God upon the wicked as being *for the sake of his name,* just as these judgments are often spoken of as being for his glory:

> **Exodus 9:16** But for this purpose I have raised you up, to show you my power, so that my name may be proclaimed in all the earth.

> **Nehemiah 9:10** [You] performed signs and wonders against Pharaoh and all his servants and all the people of his land, for you knew that they acted arrogantly against our fathers. And you made a name for yourself, as it is to this day.

The Bible also speaks along these same lines about the results and effects of his works of creation. That is, these consequences are for his name just as they are for his glory, as seen here:

> **Psalm 8:1** O LORD, our Lord, how majestic is your name in all the earth! You have set your glory above the heavens.

After saying this the psalmist then makes many observations about God's works of creation. At the end of his list, the conclusion reiterates the beginning:

> **Psalm 8:9** O LORD, our Lord, how majestic is your name in all the earth!

The next quote comes after a similar pattern of mentioning the various works of God in creation. Indeed, this Psalm provides a particularly strong list of God's creative works followed by:

> **Psalm 148:13** Let them praise the name of the LORD, for his name alone is exalted; his majesty is above earth and heaven.

All of these texts, and many others, clearly teach and imply that God created the world for the sake of his name, just as he does for his glory.

19
An Arena for His Perfections to Be Known

At this point in the work, we are unpacking Section IV of the second major division, detailing what the Bible teaches about why God made the world. Section IV deals particularly with three major purposes God had in mind for creating all things. Each of these is clear in the Bible. In the last chapter, we covered the first one, namely, that God created for the sake of his name, which means very much the same as for the sake of his glory. Now we analyze the second purpose:

> B. To make his perfections known

When God presents and shows his perfections, greatness, and excellent attributes, the Bible speaks of these manifestations in much the same way as it speaks of his glory.

For example, several passages of Scripture lead us to believe that the enjoyment of these manifestations is the great purpose God had in mind for creating *the moral world*. It seems God created moral agents so they would see God manifest his perfections, greatness, and excellent attributes, and enjoy what they see. All moral agents should, therefore, be active in fulfilling this purpose of God's for their lives.

To support this conclusion, observe a certain argument that some of God's people have made to him. These particular folks were unhappy about death or destruction coming into their lives, and they were complaining about that dreaded state of affairs to the Lord. Their argument was based on the truth that in that poor condition they would not be able to know or make known the glorious and excellent attributes of God.

Psalm 88:11-12 Is your steadfast love declared in the grave, or your faithfulness in Abaddon? Are your wonders known in the darkness, or your righteousness in the land of forgetfulness? (See also Ps 30:9; Is 38:18-19)

The argument seems to be along these lines: "Lord, why should we perish? If we do, how will your end and purpose for our existence be obtained? If we are destroyed, how will you glory be known or declared?"

The worship of God's excellent attributes and perfections is the end God had in mind for the *good part* of the moral world. In other words, the ultimate end of God's people is to see these wondrous aspects of God's being and praise him for them. When they do, they are engaged in the same thing that is meant by the phrase "bring glory to God." This is clear in Scripture:

Isaiah 43:21 The people whom I formed for myself that they might declare my praise.

1 Peter 2:9 But you are a chosen race, a royal priesthood, a holy nation, a people for his own possession, that you may proclaim the excellencies of him who called you out of darkness into his marvelous light.

According to these passages, the ultimate end of God for creating his people is that they would praise his excellent attributes. When his people do this, this is clearly what makes them *valuable* as a part of God's creation. The praise of God's perfections is the proper *fruit* that should come from their lives.

At one point in the book of Isaiah, the conversion of the Gentile nations to the one true faith is spoken of this way:

Isaiah 60:6 They. . . shall come. . . and bring good news, the praises of the LORD.

> **Isaiah 66:19** I will send... to the nations... to the coastlands afar off, that have not heard my fame or seen my glory. And they shall declare my glory among the nations.

This is also the proper tendency of true virtue. It moves in this direction precisely because this is the direction in which God created it to move. And true moral goodness rests in declaring God's glory for the same reason. It is the final destination of all truly holy dispositions:

> **1 Chronicles 16:8; 23-24** Make known his deeds among the peoples... Tell of his salvation from day to day... Declare his glory among the nations! (See also Ps 9:1-14; 19:1; 26:7; 71:18; 75:9; 76:1; 79:13; 96:2-3; 101:1; 107:22; 118:17; 145:6-12; Is 42:12; 64:1-2; Jer 31:10)

Furthermore, the manifestation and worship of God's excellent qualities and attributes is also spoken of as the ultimate end of God's *moral government*. This is true in particular of the great *judgments* he executes upon sin. Consider the following.[1]

> **Exodus 9:16** But for this purpose I have raised you up, to show you my power, so that my name may be proclaimed in all the earth.

> **Daniel 4:17** The sentence is by the decree of the watchers... to the end that the living may know that the Most High rules the kingdom of men and gives it to whom he will and sets over it the lowliest of men.

This same purpose of displaying the grandeur and wonder of God's perfections is also spoken of in Scripture as the great end of God's *works of favor and mercy to his people*. Consider these passages:

---

[1] There are so many other passages that teach this truth, they are too numerous to write them out individually. But here are some of the references for your study: Ex 14:17-18; 1 Sm 17:46; Ps 83:18; Is 45:3; Ez 6:7-14; 7:4-9, 27; 11:10-12; 12:15-20; 13:9-23; 14:8; 15:7; 21:5; 22:16; 25:7-17; 26:6; 28:22-24; 29:9-16; 30:8-26; 32:15; 33:29; 35:4-15; 38:23; 39:6-22.

> **2 Kings 19:19** So now, O LORD our God, save us, please, from his hand, that all the kingdoms of the earth may know that you, O LORD, are God alone.
>
> **1 Kings 8:59-60** May he maintain the cause of his servant and the cause of his people Israel, as each day requires, that all the peoples of the earth may know that the LORD is God; there is no other. (See also Ex 6:7; 8:22; 16:22; 1 Kgs 20:28; Ps 102:21; Ez 23:49; 24:24; 25:5; 35:9; 39:21-22.)

His glorious manifestations are also spoken of as God's ultimate end in the *eternal damnation of the wicked* and in the *eternal happiness of his righteous people:*

> **Romans 9:22-23** What if God, desiring to show his wrath and to make known his power, has endured with much patience vessels of wrath prepared for destruction, in order to make known the riches of his glory for vessels of mercy, which he has prepared beforehand for glory?

In the same way, God's display of his greatness is spoken of as the great end he has in mind for all the *miracles* he has done. This can be seen in Exodus 7:17; 8:10; 10:2, Deuteronomy 29:5-6, and Ezekiel 24:17.

God's display of his excellent qualities is also spoken of as his ultimate end for the *ordinances* he has established, such as the priesthood and the institution of the Sabbath:

> **Exodus 29:44-46** Aaron also and his sons I will consecrate to serve me as priests. I will dwell among the people of Israel and will be their God. And they shall know that I am the LORD their God.
>
> **Exodus 31:13** Above all you shall keep my Sabbaths, for this is a sign between me and you throughout your generations, that you may know that I, the LORD, sanctify you. (See also 20:12, 20)

Likewise, the display of his perfections is also the ultimate end of his work of *redeeming Israel from Egypt,* as seen in Exodus 7:5, Deuteronomy 4:34-35, and here:

> **Psalm 106:8** Yet he saved them for his name's sake, that he might make known his mighty power.

The same is true regarding God's *redemption of Israel from Babylonian captivity,* as seen here:

> **Ezekiel 20:34-38** I will bring you out from the peoples and gather you out of the countries where you are scattered. . . And I will bring you into the wilderness of the peoples, and there I will enter into judgment with you face to face. As I entered into judgment with your fathers in the wilderness of the land of Egypt. . . And I will bring you into the bond of the covenant. I will purge out the rebels from among you. . . Then you will know that I am the LORD.
>
> **Ezekiel 20:42** And you shall know that I am the LORD, when I bring you into the land of Israel.
>
> **Ezekiel 20:44** And you shall know that I am the LORD, when I deal with you for my name's sake. (See also 28:25-26; 36:11; 37:6, 13)

The glorious display of his excellent attributes is also declared to be God's ultimate end in his work of redemption through Jesus Christ. This is true both in the *purchase* of redemption as well as its *application* to God's people.

> **Romans 3:25-26** Whom God put forward as a propitiation by his blood, to be received by faith. . . It was to show his righteousness at the present time, so that he might be just and the justifier of the one who has faith in Jesus.

> **Ephesians 2:4-7** But God, being rich in mercy. . . that he might show the immeasurable riches of his grace in kindness toward us in Christ Jesus.
>
> **Ephesians 3:8-10** To preach to the Gentiles the unsearchable riches of Christ, and to bring to light for everyone what is the plan of the mystery hidden for ages in God who created all things, so that through the church the manifold wisdom of God might now be made known to the rulers and authorities in the heavenly places.
>
> **Psalm 22:21-22** Save me from the mouth of the lion. . . I will tell of your name to my brothers; in the midst of the congregation I will praise you.

Compare that passage with Hebrews 2:12 and John 17:26. And consider another to make the point clear:

> **Isaiah 64:1-2** Oh that you would rend the heavens. . . to make your name known to your adversaries!

Notice also, the manifestation of God's perfections is the ultimate end for the great, *actual salvation* he has brought about. This refers to the actual application of salvation among both Jews and Gentiles after Jesus had died on the cross to purchase it. For example:

> **Isaiah 49:22-23** I will lift up my hand to the nations. . . and they shall bring your sons in their bosom. . . Kings shall be your foster fathers. . . Then you will know that I am the LORD. (See also Ez 16:62; 29:21; 34:27; 36:38; 39:28-29 and Joel 3:17)

Furthermore, when we study God's *common providence,* we find the same reality. That is, the purpose of it is to promote and display God's excellent ways, works and attributes:

> **Job 37:6-7** For to the snow he says, "Fall on the earth," likewise to the downpour, his mighty downpour. He seals up the hand of every man, that all men whom he made may know it.

It is the same when it comes to the *Day of Judgment*. This refers to that time of grand consummation when God's moral government of the world is brought to its proper conclusion. It is the day when God brings every person to the fitting end for which he designed them. In fact, in Scripture this is called:

> **Romans 2:5** The day of wrath when God's righteous judgment will be revealed.

Finally, the *declaration* of God's perfections is spoken of in this same way. By "declaration" is meant the open display of God's excellent works and ways. This declaration is the happy result of God's work of creation:

> **Psalm 19:1-5** The heavens declare the glory of God, and the sky above proclaims his handiwork. Day to day pours out speech, and night to night reveals knowledge... In them he has set a tent for the sun, which comes out like a bridegroom leaving his chamber, and, like a strong man, runs its course with joy.

Taking all these passages seriously leads us to only one conclusion: When God manifests his perfections in the world, he does so for the sake of his own glory. This truth corresponds to and solidifies the conclusion we have already reached in this work, namely, God made himself his own ultimate end in creating the world.

20
For the Praise of His Eternal Glory

～

So far, we have deduced from Scripture two purposes God had for creating the world. First, he did it for the sake of his name, and secondly, he did it in order to have a forum for his perfections to be exercised and glorified. Here, we will look at one final purpose, namely, that he would be praised appropriately. In taking all three of these purposes together, we see them converging with one another and pointing to one ultimate end God had for creating the world, he did it for his own glory.

C. So that he will be praised

There are many passages in the Bible that speak of God's praise in the same way as it speaks of his name and glory. Many of the points listed in the previous chapter have additional scriptural support, passages that speak of the same topics discussed there. But these passages express God's end as the "praise of God," referring to it in the same way as God's name and glory.

For example, the praise of God is spoken of as the ultimate end of the *existence of God's people.* The same passage we saw before applies here as well:

> **Jeremiah 13:11** For as the loincloth clings to the waist of a man, so I made the whole house of Israel and the whole house of Judah cling to me, declares the LORD, that they might be for me a people, a name, a praise, and a glory.

Likewise, the praise of God is spoken of as his end for the moral world:

> **Matthew 21:16** Out of the mouth of infants and nursing babies you have prepared praise.

Think about this verse a moment. It means that God, in his sovereignty and wisdom, has so ordered the world of moral beings that he will obtain the great end for which his intelligent creatures are designed. They *will* praise him. His power to bring about his praise is even more especially seen when he ordains that his praise flow from those who have no real power within themselves. Infants and nursing babies are inferior and less sufficient than their adult counterparts, yet even they are made to overflow in praise to God (compare this to Psalm 8:1-2).

Now, think back to an earlier discussion. We observed an argument that some make to God concerning the possibility of their destruction or death. Remember, the argument declares that if they die, God's excellent qualities could not be made known through them. If dead or ruined, God's desired end of being praised can't be brought into being. Simply stated, God's excellent attributes will not be declared by someone who is dead.

This same argument applies not only to the declaration of God's excellent qualities, but also to his praise. When people speak this way in Scripture, it is implied that the praise of God is the ultimate end for which God made man, as seen in the following:

> **Psalm 88:10-12** Do the departed rise up to praise you? . . . Are your wonders known in the darkness?

> **Psalm 30:9** What profit is there in my death, if I go down to the pit? Will the dust praise you? Will it tell of your faithfulness?

> **Psalm 115:17-18** The dead do not praise the LORD, nor do any who go down into silence. But we will bless the LORD from this time forth and forevermore. Praise the LORD!

Isaiah 38:18-19 For Sheol does not thank you; death does not praise you; those who go down to the pit do not hope for your faithfulness. The living, the living, he thanks you.

God's praise is also spoken of as the end of the *virtue* of God's people. That is, the goodness of his people has the ultimate purpose of praising God. The Bible speaks of this in the same way as it does the glory of God:

Philippians 1:11 Filled with the fruit of righteousness that comes through Jesus Christ, to the glory and praise of God.

So it is with God's *work of redemption.* The Bible speaks of its end purpose as the praise of God as well as the glory of God.

Look again at Ephesians 1 to see this. In that chapter the various components of God's great work of redemption are listed, insisted upon, and set forth in exceedingly great glory. Then, sprinkled throughout the passage as the great end of all his work of redemption, we find that it is all "to the praise of his glory" (see verses 6, 12, and 14). Philippians 1:11 is doubtless saying the same thing, redemption is for "the glory and praise of God."

We also find an agreeable connection to this in the Old Testament. In the narrative of Jacob, we read of his fourth son, Judah. This was the son from whom the great Redeemer was to come by the special direction of God's providence. The name *Judah* means praise. This name of praise would be happily worked out in history (as the ultimate end of redemption) through one of Judah's posterity, the Messiah, Jesus Christ.

Again in the Old Testament, we find the praise of God as the ultimate end of God's willingness to forgive his people of their sins and save them. These passages indicate that God's ultimate end in forgiving his people and saving them is that he might be praised, just as his name and glory are often spoken of as the end of these things:

Isaiah 48:9-11 For my name's sake I defer my anger, for the sake of my praise I restrain it for you, that I may not cut you off. Behold, I have refined you. . . For my own sake, for my own sake, I do it, for how should my name be profaned? My glory I will not give to another.

Jeremiah 33:8-9 I will cleanse them from all the guilt of their sin. . . and I will forgive all the guilt of their sin. . . And this city shall be to me a name of joy, a praise and a glory.

Earlier we saw that the *holy part* of the moral, intelligent creatures God made expresses desire for the glory of God. The people God has redeemed delight in his glory. The holy principles at work within them have an end goal – to bring glory to God. These holy principles tend toward, reach after, and rest in this goal as their highest actions. Likewise, an abundant number of passages teach that this holy group also expresses the same desire, delight, and tending toward the *praise* of God.

There are so many passages along these lines that a seemingly endless list could be developed. Think of all the places where God's saints declared this, expressing their deep and sincere praises to God. They desired him, and they desired to praise him. They also called on all nations to praise him. In fact, they called on every being in heaven and on earth to praise him. They cried out to one another in overflowing rapture, "Hallelujah, praise the Lord. Praise him forever." They expressed their resolution to praise God as long as they lived and to praise him through all generations. Indeed, they resolved to praise him forever! Without end, they will declare how good and satisfying the praise of God is!

Finally, the praise of God is the desirable, glorious *result and effect of all his works of creation.* Here are a few passages that unfold this truth: Psalm 145:5-10, the entirety of Psalm 148, and Psalm 103:19-22.

It should be clear to the reader that when God created the world, he had in view the three purposes detailed in Section IV. First, he created that his name would be honored, secondly, to provide an arena for his perfect attributes to be seen and known, and thirdly, so that his glory would be praised appropriately. As has been shown, all three of these support the proposition I am making in this work, that God created the world ultimately for his own glory.

But the Bible speaks of another ultimate end God had in mind when he created, his great desire to shower good and benefit upon his people. Note carefully, he loves his people as an ultimate end, not a subordinate end. In Section V (covered in the next two chapters) we will look at this point and explore how the good of the creature and the glory of God are not at odds with each other.

21
THE GOOD OF THE CREATURE AND THE GLORY OF GOD

Under Section IV we discussed three major purposes God had for creating the world, all related to bringing glory and praise to himself. Now, we will move to another purpose God had for creating the world, as taught in the Bible.

Section V: The communication of good to his creatures as an ultimate end

There are several important points that need to be made about this reality. Each of these points will be supported from Scripture.

    A. The communication of good is an ultimate end.

When God *communicates good* to his creatures, this is *in itself* pleasing to God. As already discussed, this communication of good is not merely a subordinate end. It is not agreeable and valuable merely because of its relation to some further end.

In contrast, when God executes justice in punishing the sins of men, this is a subordinate end, which is agreeable and valuable because of its relationship to a further end. But it is not so with God's communication of good to his creatures, which he considers valuable on its own account. He delights in it simply and ultimately, without desiring some end beyond it.

This is true, though sometimes the Bible does refer to God as taking pleasure in bringing about punishment against the sins of men. Here are two examples:

Deuteronomy 28:63 The LORD will take delight in bringing ruin upon you and destroying you.

Ezekiel 5:13 Thus shall my anger spend itself, and I will vent my fury upon them and satisfy myself.

However, when the Scriptures speak of God bringing about goodness and showing mercy, it is spoken of in a much different way. In fact, it seems that God's delight in his manifestations of blessing and mercy are, in a certain sense, opposite of the type of delight he has in exercising wrath. His wrath is spoken of as something he approaches with a kind of backwardness and reluctance. In other words, bringing about the misery of his creatures is not agreeable to him *on its own account.* These passages will shed light on this point:

Nehemiah 9:17 You are a God ready to forgive, gracious and merciful, slow to anger and abounding in steadfast love.

Psalm 103:8 The LORD is merciful and gracious, slow to anger and abounding in steadfast love.

Psalm 145:8 The LORD is gracious and merciful, slow to anger and abounding in steadfast love. (See also Jonah 4:2)

Micah 7:18 Who is a God like you, pardoning iniquity... He does not retain his anger forever, because he delights in steadfast love.

Ezekiel 18:32 I have no pleasure in the death of anyone, declares the Lord GOD; so turn, and live.

Lamentations 3:33 He does not willingly afflict or grieve the children of men.

Ezekiel 33:11 As I live, declares the Lord GOD, I have no pleasure in the death of the wicked, but that the wicked turn from his way and live; turn back, turn back from your evil ways, for why will you die, O house of Israel?

2 Peter 3:9 The Lord is. . . not wishing that any should perish, but that all should reach repentance.

From these verses it is clear that God's communication of wrath is a subordinate end. On the other hand, his communication of his mercy and grace is an ultimate end, valued for what it is in itself without reference to any further end.

B. Redemption through Jesus is not a mere subordinate end.

Similarly, the Bible does not speak of God's *work of redemption* as something that is merely subordinate to some further end. In fact, since the redemption brought about by Christ finds its source and foundation in the grace and love of God to men, then it should be understood as a communication of the goodness of God to them. Such communication, as we have seen, is biblically considered an end in itself, valuable in its own right. Study these verses carefully:

John 3:16 For God so loved the world, that he gave his only Son, that whoever believes in him should not perish but have eternal life.

1 John 4:9-10 In this the love of God was made manifest among us, that God sent his only Son into the world, so that we might live through him. In this is love, not that we have loved God but that he loved us and sent his Son to be the propitiation for our sins.

Ephesians 2:4 But God, being rich in mercy, because of the great love with which he loved us. . .

But if God's love for his people is only given as a means to achieve some *further* end, then *that further end* would be where God's love truly terminates. Think about this a moment. If God loves people only as a way of loving something beyond them, then that thing beyond them would be the ultimate object of his love. That thing beyond them would be where his love is truly manifested, strictly and properly speaking. If his love for us is for something else other than and beyond our good (so that our good is not regarded ultimately but only subordinately), then we would be faced with a difficult reality. Our good or our interest in the sight of God would be considered *nothing* in itself, but only a means to some other end.

However, the Bible does not speak of our good in this subordinate kind of way. In fact, the Scriptures in every place describe the great things Christ did and suffered as being directly from his great love, which he showered upon us from his own heart. Here is how the apostle Paul speaks of the love of Christ for his people:

> **Galatians 2:20** [Christ] loved me and gave himself for me.
>
> **Ephesians 5:25** Husbands, love your wives, as Christ loved the church and gave himself up for her.

Here is how Jesus himself talks about this:

> **John 17:19** And for their sake I consecrate myself.

Furthermore, the Word of God pictures Christ as resting in the salvation and glory of his people, which he was ultimately (not subordinately) seeking. He rested in such a way as having reached his goal, the prize he was aiming at. When Christ rested in his redeemed people, it led him to actually enjoy the torture of his soul. As he suffered extreme agony and labored in death, his own soul was rewarded and satisfied, since in his suffering he was bringing about his rest in the salvation and glory of his people. Consider this passage carefully:

> **Isaiah 53:10-11** When his soul makes an offering for sin, he shall see his offspring; he shall prolong his days; the will of the LORD shall prosper in his hand. Out of the anguish of his soul he shall see and be satisfied; by his knowledge shall the righteous one, my servant, make many to be accounted righteous, and he shall bear their iniquities.

Here, Christ is pictured as seeing beforehand the agony his soul must endure at the cross. Through this suffering, however, he saw his "offspring." These are the people redeemed as a result of his pain. This passage implies that the most true and proper delight Christ enjoys is in the process of bringing about the salvation of his church. He is not bringing about his church's salvation merely as a means to some further end! No, but his rejoicing and satisfaction is found *most directly* and properly in it.

This reality is further proven by certain passages that speak of Christ rejoicing in his bride. These texts represent Christ as the bridegroom of the bride, who labors to purchase her as his own. The fruit of his labor is union with her, and he rejoices directly in obtaining this end:

> **Isaiah 62:5** As the bridegroom rejoices over the bride, so shall your God rejoice over you.

Furthermore, the expressions recorded in Zephaniah are emphatic and strong, teaching the same truth of God's ultimate purpose and joy in the salvation of his people:

> **Zephaniah 3:17** The LORD your God is in your midst, a mighty one who will save; he will rejoice over you with gladness; he will quiet you by his love; he will exult over you with loud singing.

Along the same lines:

> **Proverbs 8:30-31** Then I was beside him, like a master workman, and I was daily his delight, rejoicing before him

always, rejoicing in his inhabited world and delighting in the children of man.

Also, there are passages that speak of the redeemed saints as God's portion, his jewels, and his special treasure. These passages abundantly confirm the point. For example, see John 12:23-32 (however, this passage contains certain elements that are best categorized beneath the next section).

C. God communicates good to his creatures for the sake of his own goodness and mercy.

God's communication of his divine goodness is sometimes referred to as being for his own *goodness'* sake or for his *mercies'* sake. This divine goodness pertains particularly to God's forgiveness of sin and provision of salvation. We should also notice that the Bible refers to these things (goodness' sake and mercies' sake) in just the same way as it refers to the sake of God's *name*.

Several passages were presented earlier that focused on forgiveness and salvation being for the sake of God's name. God brings these same things about for his own goodness' and mercies' sake as well. For example, notice the parallel between "goodness" and "name" here:

> **Psalm 25:7, 11** Remember not the sins of my youth or my transgressions; according to your steadfast love remember me, for the sake of your goodness, O LORD! . . . For your name's sake, O LORD, pardon my guilt.

Here are a few other passages that support this truth:

> **Nehemiah 9:31** Nevertheless, in your great mercies you did not make an end of them or forsake them, for you are a gracious and merciful God.

The phrase "in your great mercies" means the same as "for the sake of your mercy."

> **Psalm 6:4** Turn, O LORD, deliver my life; save me for the sake of your steadfast love.

> **Psalm 31:16** Make your face shine on your servant; save me in your steadfast love!

> **Psalm 44:26** Rise up; come to our help! Redeem us for the sake of your steadfast love!

This "steadfast love" is the same as God's mercy.

One more passage makes this point in a remarkable way. Here, God speaks of his love to the children of Israel as they wandered in the wilderness. He speaks as though his love were given for love's sake. The best way to understand this is as though God's goodness to his people were its own end and motive, not subordinate to any other end.

> **Deuteronomy 7:7-8** It was not because you were more in number than any other people that the LORD set his love on you and chose you, for you were the fewest of all peoples, but it is because the LORD loves you.

Thus, God is motivated in his works for the sake of his goodness and mercy as an ultimate end, valuable in itself without reference to any further end.

D. God's governing acts communicate his goodness.

The communication of God's goodness is also depicted in Scripture as coming through his government of every part of the world. God's eternal subjects are the ones who benefit from the goodness of his governing power. This is implied when the Bible teaches us that Christ is seated at the right hand of the Father and that he is the King over angels and men. Indeed, the Word of God informs us that Jesus is the head of the entire universe. The Father has given all power in heaven and on earth to him.

The reason he reigns in such power, Scripture teaches, is for the purpose and end of promoting the happiness of his people. He is made the head over all things for the church and holds the governing power of the whole created order for their good. These great truths are taught in Ephesians 1:20-23, John 17:2, Matthew 11:27; 28:18-19, and John 3:35.

Jesus also implies this truth when he speaks about the Son of Man being the Lord of the Sabbath:

> **Mark 2:27-28** The Sabbath was made for man, not man for the Sabbath. So the Son of Man is lord even of the Sabbath.

See how he says that "the Sabbath was made for man?" The Lord made the Sabbath *for man.* That being true, we could also argue that all things were made for man, since the Son of Man is *Lord of all things.*

Taking all these verses together, it is expressly clear in Scripture that God communicates the goodness of himself to his created moral agents as an ultimate end. He does it for its own sake, as something intrinsically valuable to him. The communication of his goodness to them is not a subordinate goal. He doesn't do it only so that he can move to some further goal.

22
THE HAPPINESS OF GOD'S PEOPLE

Here, we will continue our discussion concerning the reality that one of God's ultimate ends in creating the world was to express goodness to the creatures he has made, in order to make them truly happy. In other words, it was good and valuable (in itself) for God to communicate his goodness to them, which leads, of course, to their joy. In the previous chapter, we considered the first four points supporting this idea and showed many passages that undergird it. Now, we will continue with the fifth point:

E. God uses all creation for the good of his people.

Not only does God govern generally for the good of his people, but also he uses the whole of creation for their good. As he governs it all, his people receive incredible blessing and benefit. This is elegantly portrayed here:

> **Deuteronomy 33:26** There is none like God, O Jeshurun, who rides through the heavens to your help.

The implication of this verse is that the whole universe is a machine that God has made for his own use. He uses it for the good of his people, riding upon various aspects of it like a chariot.

The prophet Ezekiel saw this same reality in his visions (Ezekiel 1:22; 26-28). There, God was seated in heaven, governing all creation. Ezekiel observed the wheels of the great chariot, which pictured the inferior part of creation, that is, this visible universe. Like wheels, it is subject to continual changes and revolutions. As the wheels of the chariot move, the motion is a symbol of God's providence. In the constant revolutions, alterations, and all the successive events of history, God sits on his throne in the heavens. The Spirit of God reigns over these wheels from above the expanse of sky and space.

In Deuteronomy 33:26 Moses tells us why God moves the wheels of this chariot or, as it were, rides in the chariot sitting in his heavenly seat. It is all *for the salvation of his people.* This is the end toward which God is making progress in the chariot. The salvation of his people is the appointed destination of his journey.

F. God judges the wicked for the good of his people.

The Bible also teaches that God's judgments on wicked people are, in fact, for the *happiness of his people.* His judgments are a subordinate end, leading to the ultimate end of the joy of his people. The Bible speaks this way of God's judgments issued in this world as well as in the everlasting state of damnation in the world to come. Here is a verse that shows how this works in *this world:*

> **Isaiah 43:3-4** For I am the LORD your God, the Holy One of Israel, your Savior. I give Egypt as your ransom, Cush and Seba in exchange for you. Because you are precious in my eyes, and honored, and I love you, I give men in return for you, peoples in exchange for your life.

This passage teaches that God's works of vindictive justice are, as it turns out, truly works of mercy to his people. His wrath is poured out on the wicked, yes, but why? It is ultimately for the good of his children. This same truth is taught in Psalm 136:10, 15, 17-20.

Now, think about God's judgments against the wicked in the *next world,* where they will face his eternal damnation. This, too, is ultimately for the good of God's people:

> **Romans 9:22-23** What if God, desiring to show his wrath and to make known his power, has endured with much pa-

tience vessels of wrath prepared for destruction, in order to make known the riches of his glory for vessels of mercy, which he has prepared beforehand for glory.

It is evident here that God has reasons for the final destructive punishment of the wicked, as verse 22 teaches. Verse 23 then gives us another reason for this, namely, that God could *show the riches of his glory to his vessels of mercy*. That is, he gives them *higher degrees* of glory and happiness as they relish the things they enjoy through Christ.

In other words, through eternally punishing the wicked, God's people (his "vessels of mercy") enjoy a greater sense of value and greater appreciation for God's free grace bestowed upon them. If God did not eternally punish the wicked, then his redeemed people could not have the capacity to fully enjoy his mercy and grace. So eternal punishment is a subordinate end to the ultimate end of the full joy of God's redeemed people.

G. God pours out his eternal goodness.

Furthermore, it seems evident from Scripture that God's ultimate end for creating the world was to *pour out his goodness* upon the eternal subjects of his goodness. After all, the Bible teaches that all of creation is theirs, every single part of it:

> **1 Corinthians 3:21-23** For all things are yours, whether Paul or Apollos or Cephas or the world or life or death or the present or the future - all are yours. . .

Notice the universal nature of these words. The apostle Paul uses the word "all." He means for us to understand that this includes everything. Both God's works of creation and all his works of providence are included and mentioned in this text. So how should we understand this passage? Certainly, we should interpret it as meaning that God made all things and uses all things for the good and benefit of his people. How can we understand it any other way?

H. All God's works are for goodness and mercy.

Indeed, *all of God's works* are pictured as works of goodness and mercy to his people. It needs to be reiterated that this included both his works of creation and his works of providence. Psalm 136 is one place where this is clearly taught. The psalmist instructs us that God's wonderful works *in general* are for the benefit of his people:

> **Psalm 136:4** To him who alone does great wonders, for his steadfast love endures forever.

"Great wonders" speaks generally and broadly of all God's works. The psalmist further informs us that God's specific *creative* works, every part of them, are for the good and benefit of his people:

> **Psalm 136:5-9** To him who by understanding made the heavens, for his steadfast love endures forever; to him who spread out the earth above the waters, for his steadfast love endures forever; to him who made the great lights, for his steadfast love endures forever; the sun to rule over the day, for his steadfast love endures forever; the moon and stars to rule over the night, for his steadfast love endures forever.

In the rest of the Psalm, we learn this is true of God's works of *providence* as well. All of them are performed by the Lord as a means of showering goodness and benefit – "steadfast love" – upon his children. This fact moves us to the next point.

I. God's works of providence are for the good of his people.

In the following verse, we read a blessed and amazing expression which will be pronounced over God's righteous people on the Day of Judgment:

> **Matthew 25:34** Inherit the kingdom prepared for you from the foundation of the world.

This glorious statement shows God's ultimate end in creating the world, which is his people blossoming with the fruit of his goodness to them.

His goodness flows to them through his creating the world to begin with and in his providential guidance of it. In other words, all of God's works have been in preparation for this kingdom. When he laid the foundation of the world, it was ultimately for this kingdom to be granted to his people and to give them the ability to enjoy the glory of it. And everything he has providential accomplished since laying the foundation of the world has been for the same purpose.

J. The deeds of God's people fulfill his ultimate purpose.

Agreeable to the last point is this one. When God's people perform good and virtuous deeds as part of the moral world, they are fulfilling the ultimate end of virtue in that moral world. Consider these passages:

> **Romans 13:8-10** The one who loves another has fulfilled the law. The commandments, "You shall not commit adultery, You shall not murder" . . . and any other commandment, are summed up in this word: "You shall love your neighbor as yourself." Love does no wrong to a neighbor; therefore love is the fulfilling of the law.

> **Galatians 5:14** For the whole law is fulfilled in one word: "You shall love your neighbor as yourself."

> **James 2:8** If you really fulfill the royal law according to the Scripture, "You shall love your neighbor as yourself," you are doing well.

So the good of the creature is one ultimate end God has in mind in all he does. And he requires his moral agents to have the same goal, namely, doing good to their fellow moral agents. When this reality is accepted, then the previous passages can all be easily explained – love fulfills all of God's law.

If we refuse to accept this as one of God's ultimate ends, then understanding what the Holy Spirit intended to express in these passages would be very difficult. In fact, the Scripture clearly teaches that it is the spirit of all the true saints of God to chiefly prefer the welfare of God's people over their own joy. This was the attitude and spirit of Moses and the other prophets in that era. They sought the good of God's church over their own good. This was one of their ends, and it was used in their lives to regulate all their conduct. The same is true of the apostles, as when Paul writes, "For it is all for your sake" (2 Cor 4:15). And also:

> **2 Timothy 2:10** I endure everything for the sake of the elect, that they also may obtain the salvation that is in Christ Jesus with eternal glory.

What is true of the prophets and apostles should also be true of every Christian. The Scriptures indicate that every follower of Christ should be employed for the good of the church in all he does. Each particular member of the body is used for the good of the entire body (see Rom 12:4-5; Eph 4:15-16; 1 Cor 12:12, 25; and many others). In Hebrews 1:14 the Bible even teaches that the angels are continually being used by God to this same end, to benefit God's people.

This brings us to the end of Section V. Hopefully, you see how clearly the Bible teaches that one of God's ultimate ends in creating the world was to communicate goodness and benefit to the creatures he made. Later, we will see how God's ultimate end to glorify himself and his ultimate end to benefit his people are really one and the same ultimate end.

Before we get there, however, we will seek to understand more fully what the phrase "glory of God" really means. We will also consider how the phrases "glory of God" and "name of God" and "praise of God" all converge with one another, as far the scriptural use of the phrases is concerned.

23
SCRIPTURE ON THE INTERNAL GLORY OF GOD

So far in the second division of this work, we have determined what the Bible teaches as the ends God ultimately had in view when he created the world. We learned that he created for the sake of his name, in order to have an arena where his glorious attributes could be seen and praised, and so that his glory would be praised appropriately. We also learned that God had in view as an ultimate end the communication of his full goodness to his people. He labors to make them happy, not as a mere subordinate goal, but as one of his ultimate ends.

In the next three chapters, we will focus our discussion on the meanings of the biblical phrases "glory of God" and "name of God."

Section VI: A consideration of the biblical phrases "glory of God" and "name of God"

How should we understand these phrases? We will examine them one at a time.

A. Scriptural analysis of the phrase "glory of God"

First, notice that this phrase is sometimes used as a title for Jesus Christ, the second person of the Trinity. When used this way, it means that Christ is, in a very real sense, the emanating, shining glory of God. It is not necessary at this point to prove this truth from various passages of Scripture. In fact, I'd like to leave that understanding of the "glory of God" for now.

Instead, we will proceed to observe some key features found in the Hebrew word for *glory,* which is *kavod.* When we find the word *glory* in the English version of the Old Testament, it is almost always a translation of this Hebrew term.

There are two roots from which this word stems. First, many times it comes from the verb *kavad,* a word that means "to be heavy or make heavy." Secondly, it can stem from the adjective *kaved,* which simply means "heavy" or "weighty." It seems pretty clear that these are primary definitions. Sure, these terms can have other meanings, but these meanings seem to be derivative from the most basic understanding of the terms.

There is also a noun version of the term, which signifies "gravity, heaviness, greatness, and abundance." There are a large number of places where it appears in the Bible. A few references will suffice to make the point: Proverbs 27:3, 2 Samuel 14:26, 1 Kings 12:11, Psalm 38:4, and Isaiah 30:37.

Another use of the term deals with density. When we calculate the weight of a body, for example, our analysis involves two things, *density* and *magnitude.* The word is used this way in Exodus 19:6, where *anan kaved* is translated "thick cloud." The term is also used very often to describe something that is "great," as in Isaiah 32:2, Genesis 5:9, 1 Kings 10:2, 2 Kings 6:14; 18:17, Isaiah 36:2, and others.

These definitions and concepts of the Hebrew *kavod* provide the foundation for the meaning of the word *glory* when we find it used in Scripture.

Digging even deeper into the nuances of the concept, we find that sometimes the term signifies what is *internal, inherent,* or in the *possession* of a person. Other times it is used to describe an *emanation, exhibition, or communication* of this internal glory. Additionally, the concept sometimes signifies the *knowledge or understanding* of these emanations within the people who receive the communication. Finally, it can also be used to signify the *expressions* from that recipient, as he communicates his understanding and knowledge of the glory. The recipient may simply express the effect that the glory has had personally on him.

I will also note that the Greek New Testament word for *glory* agrees with the way the Old Testament uses it. The Greek word *doxa* parallels the Hebrew word *kavod* and means the same thing. This is clear when we analyze the Septuagint, which is a Greek translation of the Hebrew Old Testament. There, the translators generally use the word *doxa* for *kavod*. This fact could be abundantly proven by comparing particular places in the text where the two words parallel in this way. I will not spend the time to do that, however, because probably nobody denies this.

Now, I will proceed to show how these two words are used in Scripture. In particular I will bring to light how the Bible speaks of glory in the four ways mentioned above: (1) as internal, (2) as emanating, (3) as received in understanding, and (4) as expressed by the recipient.

1: Internal glory

In this understanding of *glory,* the word refers to what is inside the subject or to what the subject possesses or owns. When used this way, the word commonly points to the *excellent qualities* within the subject or his dignity and worthiness to be respected. So according to the Hebrew idiom, this is what is meant by the *weight* of thing. It is filled with these excellent qualities and that is why it carries weight and is considered heavy. If a thing is *light* (in this sense), then it is worthless. A light thing has no value and should be held in contempt. Study these verses:

> **Numbers 21:5** This [light] worthless food...
>
> **1 Samuel 18:23** It seem[s] to you a little [light] thing...
>
> **Judges 9:4** Worthless [light] fellows...

This last verse, along with Zephaniah 3:4, makes use of the term to refer to the low quality of the people being described, namely, that they are worthless, vain, and vile people. And in 2 Samuel 19:43, the term means "to despise." This interpretation might read "to set them aside as light." In Daniel 5:27, King Belshazzar was considered vile in the sight of God. He was represented as being "Tekel" or weighed in the balances and found *light*.

On the other hand, as the weight of a thing arises from the conjunction of its magnitude and specific gravity, so the word *glory* is often used to signify the *excellent qualities* of a person or thing. Normally, these excellent qualities are made up of the greatness or beauty of the person or thing. It is what makes him (or it) precious. Sometimes it is the conjunction of his (it's) greatness and beauty.[2]

Sometimes in the Bible, when *glory* is referred to in this internal way, what is meant is "in possession of," as opposed to "inherent." That is, the person or thing has an ownership of it rather than having it by nature. In this usage a person might be called *heavy* if he has abundant possessions. Likewise, a man who is empty and destitute might be referred to as *light*. This is why sometimes riches are referred to as *glory*. Here are a number of passages that imply these truths:

> **Genesis 31:1** And from what was our father's he has gained all this wealth [glory].
>
> **Esther 5:11** And Haman recounted to them the splendor [glory] of his riches...
>
> **Psalm 49:16-17** Be not afraid when a man becomes rich, when the glory of his house increases. For when he dies he will carry nothing away; his glory will not go down after him.
>
> **Nahum 2:9** Plunder the silver, plunder the gold! There is no end of the treasure or of the wealth [glory] of all precious things.

The term is also often used to describe both a great height of prosperity and when a person's life is filled with good things:

---

2 Take some time to study the following passages which prove this point: Ex 16:7-10; 28:2, 40; 33:18; Nm 16:19; Dt 5:24; 28:58; 2 Sm 6:20; 1 Chr 16:24; Est 1:4; Jb 29:20; Ps 19:1; 45:13; 63:2-3; 66:2-3; 72:19; 87:3; 102:16; 145:5-13; Is 4:2; 10:18; 17:4; 35:2-3; 40:5; 60:13; 62:2; Ez 31:18; Hb 2:14; Hg 2:3, 9; Mt 6:29; 16:27; 24:30; Lk 9:31-32; Jn 1:14; 2:11; 11:40; Rom 6:4; 1 Cor 2:8; 15:40; 2 Cor 3:10; Eph 3:21; Col 1:11; 2 Thes 1:9; Ti 2:13; 1 Pt 1:24; 2 Pt 1:17.

Genesis 45:13 You must tell my father of all my honor [glory] in Egypt.

Job 19:9 He has stripped from me my glory.

Isaiah 10:3 Where will you leave your wealth [glory]?

Isaiah 10:16 Therefore the Lord GOD of hosts will send wasting sickness among his stout warriors, and under his glory a burning will be kindled, like the burning of fire.

Isaiah 17:3-4 . . . The kingdom [will disappear] from Damascus; and the remnant of Syria will be like the glory of the children of Israel. . . And in that day the glory of Jacob will be brought low, and the fat of his flesh will grow lean.

Isaiah 21:16 All the glory of Kedar will come to an end.

Isaiah 61:6 You shall eat the wealth of the nations, and in their glory you shall boast.

Isaiah 66:11-12 That you may nurse. . . with delight from her glorious abundance. . . I will extend peace to her like a river, and the glory of the nations like an overflowing stream.

Hosea 9:11 Ephraim's glory shall fly away like a bird.

Matthew 4:8 . . . Showed him all the kingdoms of the world and their glory.

Luke 24:26 Was it not necessary that the Christ should suffer these things and enter into his glory?

John 17:22 The glory that you have given me I have given to them.

Romans 5:1-2 And we rejoice in hope of the glory of God.

Romans 8:18 The sufferings of this present time are not worth comparing with the glory that is to be revealed to us. (See also Rom 2:7, 10; 3:23; 9:23)

1 Corinthians 2:7 [A] hidden wisdom of God, which God decreed before the ages for our glory.

2 Corinthians 4:17 . . . Preparing for us an eternal weight of glory beyond all comparison.

Ephesians 1:18 . . . What are the riches of his glorious inheritance in the saints. . .

1 Peter 4:13 But rejoice insofar as you share Christ's sufferings, that you may also rejoice and be glad when his glory is revealed.

1 Peter 1:8 Rejoice with joy that is inexpressible and filled with glory.

From all these passages (and many others: Col 1:27; 3:4; 1 Thes 2:12; 2 Thes 2:14; 1 Tm 3:16; 2 Tm 2:10; Heb 2:10; 1 Pt 1:11, 21; 5:1; 2 Pt 1:3; Rv 21:24, 26; Ps 73:24; 149:5; Is 11:10), Scripture proves that *glory* is the type of thing that can be internal to a subject. In the next chapter, we will show from the Bible how *glory* can also be an emanation (or communication) from the subject outward to others.

24
SCRIPTURE ON THE COMMUNICATED GLORY OF GOD

Having seen what it means that God's glory begins internal to his being, we now look at the notion that his glory extends out from his being to others. It is a communicated glory.

2: Communicated glory

As already stated, the term *glory* not only refers to what is internal to the subject (or possessed by the subject), but also very often signifies a visible exhibition of that glory. It might be in the shining brightness of the glory, when the brilliant radiance emanates in beams of light. This is why the brightness of the sun, moon, and stars is referred to as their "glory" in 1 Corinthians 15:41. But in particular, this type of usage is often seen as a way to refer to God and Christ as their glory shines outward:

> **Ezekiel 1:28** Like the appearance of the bow that is in the cloud on the day of rain, so was the appearance of the brightness all around. Such was the appearance of the likeness of the glory of the LORD.
>
> **Ezekiel 10:4** The glory of the LORD went up from the cherub to the threshold of the house, and the house was filled with the cloud, and the court was filled with the brightness of the glory of the LORD.
>
> **Isaiah 6:1-3** I saw the Lord sitting upon a throne, high and lifted up; and the train of his robe filled the temple. Above him stood the seraphim. . . And one called to another and

said: "Holy, holy, holy is the LORD of hosts; the whole earth is full of his glory!"

Compare those words with these:

John 12:41 Isaiah said these things because he saw his glory and spoke of him.

Ezekiel 43:2 And behold, the glory of the God of Israel was coming from the east. . . And the earth shone with his glory.

Isaiah 24:23 Then the moon will be confounded and the sun ashamed, for the LORD of hosts reigns on Mount Zion and in Jerusalem, and his glory will be before his elders.

Isaiah 60:1-2 Arise, shine, for your light has come, and the glory of the LORD has risen upon you. For behold, darkness shall cover the earth, and thick darkness the peoples; but the LORD will arise upon you, and his glory will be seen upon you.

Compare that passage with this one, a few verses later:

Isaiah 60:19 The sun shall be no more your light by day, nor for brightness shall the moon give you light; but the LORD will be your everlasting light, and your God will be your glory.

And a few verses from the New Testament:

Luke 2:9 The glory of the Lord shone around them.

Acts 22:11 And since I could not see because of the brightness of that light. . .

The apostle Paul refers to the shining of Moses' face as "the glory" of his countenance (2 Corinthians 3:7). Compare that with his words in that same chapter:

> **2 Corinthians 3:18** And we all, with unveiled face, beholding the glory of the Lord, are being transformed into the same image from one degree of glory to another.

In relation to the blindness of unbelievers, the same thought is found early in the next chapter:

> **2 Corinthians 4:4** To keep them from seeing the light of the gospel of the glory of Christ, who is the image of God.

Then two verses later:

> **2 Corinthians 4:6** For God, who said, "Let light shine out of darkness," has shone in our hearts to give the light of the knowledge of the glory of God in the face of Jesus Christ.

The same idea is seen here:

> **Hebrews 1:3** He is the radiance of the glory of God. . .

Next, the apostle Peter recounts his experience at the Mount of Transfiguration. He and the other disciples witnessed the incredibly bright emanation of God's glory there. They saw the bright cloud that overshadowed them as well as the way Christ's face shone with light. Peter says of this event:

> **2 Peter 1:17** For when he received honor and glory from God the Father, and the voice was borne to him by the Majestic Glory, "This is my beloved Son, with whom I am well pleased."

Here are a few verses from Revelation demonstrating the same truth:

> **Revelation 18:1** After this I saw another angel coming down from heaven, having great authority, and the earth was made bright with his glory.

> **Revelation 21:11** Having the glory of God, its radiance like a most rare jewel, like a jasper, clear as crystal.

> **Revelation 21:23** And the city has no need of sun or moon to shine on it, for the glory of God gives it light.

There are many more passages that speak of glory as the shining brilliance of light that emanates forth from the subject, including Ex 16:10; 24:16; 24:17; 33:22–23; 40:34–35; Lv 9:6; 9:23; Nm 14:10; 16:19; 1 Kgs 8:11; 2 Chr 5:14; 7:1–3; Is 58:8; Ez 3:23; 8:4; 9:3; 10:18–19; 11:22–23; 43:4–5; 44:4; Acts 7:55; Rv 15:8.

Sometimes the word *glory* (when used to describe God or Christ) contains the idea of the various communications of the fullness of God. When used this way, it means basically the same thing as God's abundant goodness and grace. In other words, the glory of God often shines from him to others in the form of his mercy, grace, and goodness, as these passages indicate:

> **Ephesians 3:16** That according to the riches of his glory he may grant you to be strengthened with power through his Spirit in your inner being.

The expression, "according to the riches of his glory," has a parallel earlier in Ephesians 1:7, with a slight difference, "according to the riches of his *grace.*" However, the two phrases seem to be equivalent in meaning, as here:

> **Ephesians 2:7** . . . The immeasurable riches of his grace in kindness toward us in Christ Jesus.

Glory is used in the same way in these two passages:

> **Philippians 4:19** And my God will supply every need of yours according to his riches in glory in Christ Jesus.

> **Romans 9:23** In order to make known the riches of his glory for vessels of mercy...

The context of this verse in Romans is important. The apostle Paul describes how God is making known two things, his *great wrath* and his *rich grace*. His great wrath is poured out upon the vessels of his wrath, as verse 22 describes. But his rich grace, which he calls the "riches of his glory," is showered upon the vessels of mercy, as verse 23 describes.

We can observe this same understanding of *glory* from the following texts:

> **Exodus 33:18** Moses said, "Please show me your glory."

When God granted Moses' request to see glory, he did it by displaying his goodness:

> **Exodus 33:19** I will make all my goodness pass before you... (See the entire context, Ex 33:18-19)

Dr. Thomas Goodwin made an observation in one of his sermons that supports this understanding of God's glory emanating in the form of mercy and goodness.[3] Here is a paraphrase of his quote:

> The Scripture speaks of God granting his people the "riches of his glory" in Ephesians 3:16. But it is primarily God's mercy that is meant by this phrase. After all, mercy is what God bestows upon his people, and it is what the Apostle was praying for in the context of the passage (see v.14). The rea-

---

[3] This sermon can be found in Volume 1, Part 2 of his works (on page 166).

son he refers to God's mercy as his glory is because mercy is the highest and most excellent quality in the character of God. He, likewise, makes this same connection elsewhere. Compare Ephesians 3:16 with Romans 9:22-23 to see this. In this latter passage, Paul speaks of God's willingness to make known the power of his wrath (in v.22). But when it comes to God's mercy, Paul writes that God desires to make known the riches of his glory on the vessels of mercy (in v.23).

To further support this, look carefully at John 12:23-32. This passage bears particularly on the point that God's glory is often referred to as a communication of his fullness, especially his goodness and mercy. When we analyze this text, focused on the words and behavior of Christ, two important arguments present themselves.

First, the happiness and salvation of human beings was an end that Christ was ultimately aiming at in his labor and sufferings.

This relates to a point we have already worked through (Second Division, Section III). There we observed that the prospect of God's glory was the thing that comforted Christ as he approached his crucifixion and other sufferings. The thought of *bringing glory to God* gave Jesus the peace he needed to face the most extreme difficulties of his mission. After all, bringing glory to God was the ultimate end of his redemptive work.

In John 12 Jesus found the same kind of comfort from the prospect of obtaining the *salvation of men*. Notice, these two comforting realities happened within Christ at exactly the same time and manner. The great end of his labor and sufferings as he died was both the *glory of God* and the *salvation of man*. Both of these thoughts brought satisfaction to his soul as he dealt with the prospect of his coming painful suffering. Take some time in John 12 to compare verses 23-24, 28-29, and 31-32.

Secondly, these two things (the glory of God and the salvation of man) were spoken of by Christ in such a way that it would be very unnatural to interpret him as referring to two distinct things.

This second argument indicates that the glory of God and its emanations and fruits, which are most notably seen in his grace to save man, should not be understood as being separate items. The connection between them is deep and organic. What he said of the salvation of human beings seems to be an exegesis (so to speak) of the glory of God. In other words, the salvation of man is the working out and unfolding of the glory of God.

In the passage Jesus spoke first about his own glory and his Father's glory. This is the ultimate end that would be obtained in his suffering and death. Then he explained and amplified what he meant, expressing how the *salvation of human beings* would be obtained in the process:

> **John 12:23** The hour has come for the Son of Man to be glorified.

Then he detailed *how* he would be glorified, bringing to light the content of his glory:

> **John 12:24** Truly, truly, I say to you, unless a grain of wheat falls into the earth and dies, it remains alone; but if it dies, it bears much fruit.

The death of the seed brings "much fruit." So the bearing of an *abundance of fruit* is the *glory* of the seed. A multitude of redeemed people is the fruit that springs from Christ's death. This multitude of his people is his glory. Remember how the church is often referred to as the glory and fullness of Christ? We see the same idea here, this time relative to the Father's glory in the salvation of his people:

> **John 12:27-28** "Now is my soul troubled. And what shall I say? 'Father, save me from this hour'? But for this purpose I have come to this hour. Father, glorify your name." Then a

voice came from heaven: "I have glorified it, and I will glorify it again."

The Father's words gave Jesus assurance and brought great comfort to his soul. In fact, he even experienced extreme joy as he thought of his approaching sufferings.

In the next verses, Jesus explained what all this glory to God consists of or what makes it up. He was showing how he could find such comfort for his soul in such dire circumstances. Look at the text, which begins with confusion caused by the voice from heaven:

> **John 12:29** The crowd that stood there and heard it said that it had thundered. Others said, "An angel has spoken to him."

Then Christ explained what the voice from heaven truly meant:

> **John 12:30-32** Jesus answered, "This voice has come for your sake, not mine. Now is the judgment of this world; now will the ruler of this world be cast out. And I, when I am lifted up from the earth, will draw all people to myself."

It is clear that the *glory* of Christ and the Father is unfolded and honored mainly in his expressions of *divine grace*. Our Redeemer made this clear by his behavior and speech in this passage. In other words, the sanctification and happiness of God's redeemed people *are the very things* that bring God and Christ glory and joy:

> **Hebrews 12:2** ... Jesus... who for the joy that was set before him endured the cross, despising the shame...

This glory, received through redeeming people, was the ultimate end Christ had in mind as he endured his sufferings. It was obtaining this glory as his end that brought satisfaction to his soul. This agrees with Isaiah's prophecy concerning why Christ would suffer:

> **Isaiah 53:10-11** Yet it was the will of the LORD to crush him; he has put him to grief... Out of the anguish of his soul he shall see and be satisfied; by his knowledge shall the righteous one, my servant, make many to be accounted righteous, and he shall bear their iniquities.

These ideas agree with the earlier observation that God's glory is like flowing light and is often represented this way. His glory is an emanation or a brilliant movement and communication of the light which flows from the luminous fountain of his being. Can any other visual picture represent his glory better? The idea that God's glory flows forth in radiant abundance from his infinite fullness of good is a natural and apt representation of how his glory is communicated. This is why in the Bible *light* is often used to represent comfort, joy, happiness, and general goodness. For example:

> **Isaiah 6:3** Holy, holy, holy is the LORD of hosts; the whole earth is full of his glory!

A better translation of the original Hebrew is, "His glory is the fullness of the whole earth." This way of understanding these words signifies much more than, "the whole earth is full of his glory." When understood properly, this verse implies that the full holiness and happiness of man is found only in the glory of God. God's glory, which is especially made up of *his* holiness, is the very thing that brings holiness and happiness to human beings. So when people truly see this glory, when it is communicated to them in a radiant flowing fashion, they find and become the fullness of what God means for them to be.

Also in this verse, the glory of God seems to be referring to the radiant, brilliant, flowing beams of light that filled the temple on that occasion. These beams of light signified God's glory shining outward, being communicated. These brilliant beams of holy light provide intelligent creatures with the full measure of holiness and happiness they were created to enjoy, since they have no fullness of these things on their own.

In conclusion, we have seen that God's glory is both internal and communicated. In both cases, this glory is something God values in itself, not for some further end. Next, we will consider the third aspect of God's glory, namely, that it should be both seen and praised.

25
VIEWING AND PRAISING GOD'S GLORY

So far, we have seen how the term *glory* has been used in Scripture to refer to God's internal glory, which he possesses in his own being. We have also seen how God communicates his glory in radiant beams of light, which very often take the form of his acts of goodness, mercy, and grace to people. Now, consider what happens when intelligent creatures find themselves immersed in those flowing beams of radiant light.

3: Received and viewed glory

God's glory is being exhibited, and people should behold it. The flowing bright light of God's glory emanates outward and finds a relationship with the eyes of recipients. As they see and behold his glory, they obtain *knowledge* of God's excellent qualities as a result. This point has to do with both *seeing* God's glory and *knowing* God as a result.

Generally speaking, light has these same qualities about it. That is, it is connected to seeing and knowing. For example, we see a luminous object by the light that flows from it.

In the Bible, knowledge is often expressed in terms of light. To see this, remember that often in Scripture the term *glory* implies *honor*. This is clear to anyone who will take some time to study a concordance. We see this connection particularly in Hebrews 3:3. There, the author states that Jesus is worthy of more "glory" than Moses. In this verse the term *glory* obviously refers to honor. Notice how the honor implies *knowledge* of the dignity and excellent qualities of the one who has the honor.

This connection between glory, honor, and knowledge is especially true when the word *glory* is applied to God:

> **Numbers 14:21** But truly, as I live. . . all the earth shall be filled with the glory of the LORD.

Based on the context, here is a paraphrase of that verse: "Every inhabitant of earth will see the manifestations I will make of my perfect holiness. They will also see my hatred of sin displayed before them. And so they will observe my infinite excellence." We see the same idea here:

> **Ezekiel 39:21-23** And I will set my glory among the nations, and all the nations shall see my judgment that I have executed, and my hand that I have laid on them. The house of Israel shall know that I am the LORD their God. . . And the nations shall know that the house of Israel went into captivity for their iniquity.

This same truth is clear in many other places in the Bible. We often read of God glorifying himself or of his being glorified. One thing is intended in these passages, that God is *making known* his divine greatness and excellent attributes to people. They can receive and see his glory, and they can know him as a result.

This brings us to the fourth aspect of God's glory, it is also to be praised. It begins internal in the being of God, then flows forth in brilliant communications from him. From this radiant flowing, his glory is received and observed by his created beings, leading them to know him. Once this happens, it only makes sense that they would praise his glory and value it supremely.

4: Praised glory

The point was just made that *glory* often signifies *honor*, which is much the same thing as *praise*. They both mean to view with high esteem and to express this high esteem in words and actions. Furthermore, it is clear that in the Bible the words *glory* and *praise* are often used as equivalent expressions, as these passages indicate:

Psalm 50:23 The one who offers thanksgiving [praise]. . . glorifies me.

Psalm 22:23 You who fear the LORD, praise him! All you offspring of Jacob, glorify him.

Isaiah 42:8 My glory I give to no other, nor my praise to carved idols.

Isaiah 42:12 Let them give glory to the LORD, and declare his praise in the coastlands.

Isaiah 48:9-11 For my name's sake I defer my anger, for the sake of my praise I restrain it for you. . . For my own sake I do it, for. . . My glory I will not give to another.

Jeremiah 13:11 That they might be for me a people, a name, a praise, and a glory.

Ephesians 1:6 To the praise of his glorious grace.

Ephesians 1:12 To the praise of his glory. (See also Eph 1:14)

Philippians 1:11 That comes through Jesus Christ, to the glory and praise of God.

2 Corinthians 4:15 That as grace extends to more and more people it may increase thanksgiving, to the glory of God.

From these examples, it is clear that the phrase *praise of God* implies a high esteem of God and a real love for him in the heart. To praise God is to allow thoughts of him to have highest priority in the mind, to purposefully exalt our thoughts of him above all other thoughts, and to find our greatest joy in all of his excellent qualities and perfections.

Any person who is acquainted with the Bible sees these facts clearly. However, some readers may need to be further satisfied that this is what the Bible teaches. There are an innumerable number of passages that teach these truths. Among them are these: Ps 145:1–12; 34:1–3; 44:8; 71:14–15; 99:2–3; 107:31–32; 108:3–5; 119:164; 148:13; 150:2; Rv 19:1–3.

Furthermore, the phrase *praise of God* also implies joy in God. When a person praises God, he is *rejoicing* in his perfections. You can see this connection here:

> **Psalm 33:1-2** Shout for joy in the LORD, O you righteous!
> Praise befits the upright.

Plenty of other passages serve the purpose of showing this as well, including: Ps 9:1–14; 28:7; 35:27–28; 42:4; 63:5; 67:3–5; 71:22–23; 104:33–34; 106:47; 135:3; 147:1; 149:1–6; Acts 2:46–47; 3:8; Rv 19:6–7.

Additionally, how often do we read of *singing praise?* Singing is an expression of joy. The Bible speaks of it as making a joyful noise. Many times it is used in Scripture to imply gratitude and love to God for his benefits to us (Ps 30:12; 35:18; 63:3-4; 66:8-9; 71:6-8; 79:13; 98:4-5; 100:4; 107:21-22; 138:2; and many other places).

This brings us to the end of our discussion on the meaning of the phrase *the glory of God*. We have clearly seen its four basic meanings (internal, communicated, seen/known, and praised) from various places in Scripture. We now move to the second part of this section:

B. Scriptural analysis of the phrase "name of God"

It has already been indicated that in the Scripture, God's name and God's glory mean much the same thing. For example, just as *the glory of God* is sometimes used to signify the second person of the Trinity, so *the name of God* can be used in the same way.

If needed we could prove this from all of Scripture. However, the reality that these two terms are equal in meaning, power, and force in all of

Scripture can be shown from a few representative passages. First, notice here what Moses requested from God:

> **Exodus 33:18** Moses said, "Please show me your glory."

Then notice what God proclaimed in response to Moses' request:

> **Exodus 33:19** I . . . will proclaim before you my name "The LORD."

Several verses from the Psalms prove this point as well:

> **Psalm 8:1** O LORD. . . how majestic is your name in all the earth! You have set your glory above the heavens.

> **Psalm 79:9** Help us, O God of our salvation, for the glory of your name; deliver us, and atone for our sins, for your name's sake!

> **Psalm 102:15** Nations will fear the name of the LORD, and all the kings of the earth will fear your glory.

> **Psalm 148:13** His name alone is exalted; his majesty [glory] is above earth and heaven.

Here are some passages from elsewhere proving the same point:

> **Isaiah 48:9** For my name's sake I defer my anger, for the sake of my praise I restrain it for you.

> **Isaiah 48:11** For my own sake, for my own sake, I do it, for how should my name be profaned? My glory I will not give to another.

> **Isaiah 59:19** They shall fear the name of the LORD from the west, and his glory from the rising of the sun.

> **Jeremiah 13:11** That they might be for me a people, a name, a praise, and a glory, but they would not listen.

These passages make clear the strong equality between *glory* and *name*. In addition, both terms often imply the manifestation or knowledge of some excellent quality. In other words, both terms speak to the idea of someone's honor being highly publicized in the world. Here are some examples of this:

> **Genesis 11:4** Let us make a name for ourselves.

> **Deuteronomy 26:19** And that he will set you in praise and in fame [name] and in honor high above all nations. (See also 2 Sm 7:9; 8:13; 23:18; Neh 9:10; Jb 18:17; Prv 22:1.)

Now, just like *glory* and *name* have much the same meaning, so also does *praise* and *name*. Many of the places in Scripture just mentioned show this (for example, Is 48:9, Jer 13:11, and Dt 26:19). Additionally, we see it in these verses:

> **Jeremiah 33:9** And this city shall be to me a name of joy, a praise and a glory before all the nations of the earth who shall hear of all the good that I do for them.

> **Zephaniah 3:20** For I will make you renowned [a name] and praised among all the peoples of the earth.

Plus, it seems evident that God's name is often used to describe the expression or exhibition of God's goodness, as here:

> **Exodus 33:19** I will make all my goodness pass before you and will proclaim before you my name "The LORD."

And:

> **Exodus 34:5-7** The LORD descended in the cloud and stood with him there, and proclaimed the name of the LORD. The LORD passed before him and proclaimed, "The LORD, the LORD, a God merciful and gracious, slow to anger, and abounding in steadfast love and faithfulness, keeping steadfast love for thousands. . ."

The same is true of the pillar of cloud that appeared to the Israelites in the wilderness and that dwelt above the mercy seat in the tabernacle and, later, the temple. It was an illustrious and brightly emanating flow of light (or rather it represented God's spiritual, divine brightness and flowing brilliant light). This pillar of cloud is often called *the glory of the Lord,* but is also often referred to as *the name of the Lord.* Because God's glory was to dwell in the tabernacle in this way, he made a promise:

> **Exodus 29:43** There I will meet with the people of Israel, and it shall be sanctified by my glory.

Later, the temple was called the house of God's glory (see Isaiah 60:7). But the same is true of God's name, which is also said to dwell in the sanctuary. We often read that this is the place God chose to put his name. In the Hebrew it states that God caused his name to inhabit that place, to literally live in it. Sometimes modern translators of the Bible render it that way as well. For example:

> **Deuteronomy 12:11** Then to the place that the LORD your God will choose, to make his name dwell there.

The temple was built for this very purpose. This truth is supported by Psalm 74:7, where it says the temple is the "dwelling place of your name." And the mercy seat in the temple was called the throne of God's name, which in the following passage is parallel with his glory:

Jeremiah 14:21 Do not spurn us, for your name's sake; do not dishonor your glorious throne; remember and do not break your covenant with us.

We have already considered a number of biblical passages concerning these parallels in the previous sections. As you continue to mediate on these passages, it should become clear to you that ultimately God had only one ultimate end in mind in creating the world. His glory, name, and praise all mean the same thing and are all pointing to the same place. His love for his creatures also points to the exact same place. In the next and final section of this work, I hope to show how all of God's ends converge into one supreme end.

26
GOD'S ULTIMATE END IS ONE

The next two chapters will be used to cover the last major section of this work. Here, I hope to bring everything that has been covered together into a conclusion. Remember the question before us: Why did God created the world? In particular I want to show that God had:

Section VII: Only one ultimate end and what it is

It seems clear that in the Scriptures the Holy Spirit desired to represent God's ultimate end as one, not many. This is the point observed in the previous sections, and it seems especially true when the various parts of Scripture are compared with the other parts and weighed against one another.

Though this ultimate end is identified by various names, these do not appear to be names of *different* things. Rather, the variety of names signifies that these are things which all involve each other in their meanings. They are either different names for the *same thing,* or they are names of several parts of *one whole.* Or perhaps we should understand them as all describing the same whole, albeit through different lights, shades, or in its different respects and relations. This makes the most sense of the biblical data we have.

It appears that when the Bible speaks of the ultimate end of God's work, it can always be summarized by the one phrase – *the glory of God.* This phrase is the most common way Scripture describes God's ultimate end. It also seems to be the best way to describe it from the big-picture perspective. A bit of elaboration will help show this.

A. God's internal glory and external glory are the same glory.

When we speak of *the glory of God* as the ultimate end of all God's works, we need an accurate understanding of what we mean by the phrase. In using it in this context, the glory of God is the emanation and true external expression of God's internal glory and fullness. It is the outward, radiant flow and communication of the holy, eternal being of God.

In thinking of God this way, we aptly use the term *fullness*. We've already discussed what is meant by this term, but to summarize, God's fullness is his internal glory overflowing in a true and accurate exhibition. It is the external existence of his internal glory.

There is a degree of obscurity in these definitions. This is a reality that must be confessed. However, perhaps the obscurity is unavoidable. Perhaps the imperfection of language prohibits the full and clear expression of things as deeply sublime as these. Thus we may get closer to an accurate understanding if we use a variety of expressions and if we consider these things in parts. No short definition will help as much as broad, bit-by-bit, and careful examination.

Summary of the two aspects of God's glory

First, God's glory includes the proper effect that is generated when God exercises his perfections. It glorifies him when he acts outwardly on the basis of what he is inwardly.

This fact stands in opposition to the idea of God's perfections lying eternally dormant, never being used, and never bringing various effects into being. Suppose his power was eternally silent, still, and fruitless. Suppose his wisdom was eternally ineffectual, producing nothing that demonstrated his wisdom, bringing about nothing in his perfectly prudential way. Suppose all his other perfections were just as silent and ineffectual. What glory is there in that? So the glory of God most certainly includes his actions and the effects his actions produce.

Second, the phrase *glory of God* also includes the manifestation of God's internal glory to created beings. This refers to God's communicating himself, in all his infinite fullness, to the creatures he has made. It also includes the proper response of these beings as they express their high esteem and love for God, finding their rest and joy in him.

Further explanation of the oneness of God's internal and external glory

Now at first view, these two things might appear to be two entirely distinct things. But upon closer examination, it is clear that they are but one thing, being seen from various perspectives and relationships. When God exercises his perfections in order to produce a proper effect, this is not something distinct from the emanation or communication of his internal fullness to his creatures. These are both the same emanation of God's glory. They are both ways in which the excellent brightness and fullness of God's divinity are diffused and enlarged, overflowing forth from his being, or simply God's glory *existing ad extra!*

So truly, there is nothing more to God's effectual exertion of his perfection then the emanation of his internal glory to his creatures. The phrase *glory of God* is a big-picture description of this entire process.

Think now of God's *internal* glory, which is his understanding and his will. The fullness of God's understanding is referred to as his knowledge. The internal glory and fullness of God in relation to his will is referred to as his holiness and happiness. So the whole of God's internal good and glory consists in these three things: his infinite knowledge, his infinite *holiness* (or virtue), and his infinite *happiness* (or joy).

When it comes to God, there are a great many attributes within him, at least according to our way of conceiving God. But all his attributes can be summarized beneath these three. The other attributes besides these speak more of certain degrees, circumstances, or relationships.

For example, when we speak of God's power, it is a description of the degree with which he possesses knowledge, holiness, and happiness. The same is true when we speak of his infinity. Infinity is not a separate kind of good, but rather an expression of the degree of good that is in God. Likewise, God's eternity is not a distinct good he possesses, but rather the duration of the good he possesses. Again, the same is true of his immutability, which means the good he is and has never changes.

So the fullness of the Godhead means the fullness of his understanding (consisting of his knowledge) and the fullness of his will (consisting of his virtue and happiness). This being the case, when we speak of God's *external* glory, we are referring to God's communication of these three things.

When it comes to his communication of knowledge, it chiefly means his giving knowledge of himself to others. The knowledge of God is, after all, the main area of knowledge needed in order to understand the fullness of God. Therefore, the manifestation of God's glory to the minds of his creatures, so that they see and know it, is not somehow a separate thing from the overall emanation of God's fullness. This knowledge, imparted from God's internal glory to the understandings of his creatures, is part of the overall glory being communicated from him to them. Thus it is part of the one thing implied by the phrase *glory of God.*

Likewise, the communication of God's holiness or virtue is done principally by communicating how he loves himself and how others should love him. Since God is the highest of all beings, then true holiness comes when he is highly esteemed and loved. This reality is part of the communication of God's fullness, not a distinct process from it. When created beings see God's excellent qualities and come to know them and also to supremely esteem and love him because of these qualities, then holiness and true virtue become a reality.

Finally, when God communicates his joy and happiness to people, he is not communicating something different than the fullness of his being. This joy and happiness is primarily what comes from a deep *rejoicing in God,* that is, in his glorious and excellent qualities. Indeed, these glorious and excellent qualities are what God himself primarily rejoices in. If these are the things that make God happy, then these are the same things that will make his creatures happy.

To summarize, when God's creatures *know* his excellent qualities, *love* him for possessing these qualities, and *rejoice* in him, they are properly exercising and expressing honor and praise to him. But all of this can be further summarized under the one phrase, *the glory of God,* which consists in the emanation of his internal glory. We must understand this point well! There are many various aspects of this process, but all of them are signified by God's glory. After all, according to Scripture, God's glory is the one ultimate end of all his works.

That said, it is clear that God's internal and essential glory is the greatest aspect of his glory and has no variety within it. This one internal glory, though only one thing with no variations, is yet partly in God's understanding and partly in his will. The aspect that is seated in his will implies both his holiness and happiness, both of which are to be understood as his glory. Thus God's one internal glory is understood in these many aspects. And his one internal glory is what emanates into his external glory. Therefore, these many aspects of his internal glory should necessarily be understood as part of his external glory as well.

Thus God's external glory is truly only one thing as well. The appearance of it as a multiplicity of things with variety and distinction arises necessarily because of the way man receives them. The creature has distinct faculties and receives the communication from God according to these faculties.

Man was created by God in his image and so has those same two faculties which God possesses, understanding and will. God communicates himself to the understanding of the creature, giving him the *knowledge* of his glory. God also communicates himself to the will of man, giving him *holiness,* which is primarily the love of God. Also to the will God gives *happiness,* which is primarily made up of joy in God.

Though these may appear to man as separate things, they are the sum of the emanation of God's divine fullness. In the Bible they are together called *the glory of God.* The first part of this glory (knowledge) is called truth, while the second part (holiness and happiness) is called grace. So we read:

> **John 1:14** We have seen his glory, glory as of the only Son from the Father, full of grace and truth.

This verse brings it all together. We see in Scripture that the ultimate end of all God's work is one thing, and it is called the glory of God. Though his glory is expressed in many varied ways, the Scriptures most commonly refer to it in this most proper and comprehensive way, with the phrase *glory of God.*

The sun and its beams as an illustration

It is fitting to compare this glory to a radiant, flowing emanation of light coming from a bright luminary. Light is the external expression of the excellence of a luminary, exhibiting and manifesting the luminary's qualities.

Consider the sun. Countless human beings partake of its beams and enjoy its fullness. But how can so many people enjoy its radiant beams? They do it by basking in its light. The sun provides an abundant and extensive emanation and communication of itself to earth, and by means of this flowing light, the sun itself can be seen. Because of its emanation, the glory of the sun can be examined and its qualities discovered. And the emanation of this glory is what gives all the objects surrounding the sun their luster, beauty, and brightness. The communication of the internal glory of the sun is what provides all nature with life, comfort, and joy.

It is the same with the light of God. In fact, light is used often in the Bible to signify knowledge, holiness, and happiness. Some verses that use light to refer to knowledge (or the means by which knowledge is received) include Psalm 19:8; 119:105, 130, Proverbs 6:23, Isaiah 8:20; 9:2; 29:18, and Daniel 5:11. It is also used this way in many places in the New Testament, including:

> **Ephesians 5:13** But when anything is exposed by the light, it becomes visible, for anything that becomes visible is light.

"Light" is also used to signify holiness, virtue, and moral grounding, as in: Jb 25:5; Eccl 8:1; Is 5:20; 24:23; 62:1; Ez 28:17; Dn 2:37; 1 Jn 1:5; and many others. It also is used abundantly to indicate comfort, joy, and happiness: Est 8:16; Jb 18:18; 22:28; 29:3; 30:26; Ps 27:1; 97:11; 118:27;

112:4; Is 42:16; 50:10; 59:9; Jer 13:16; Lam 3:2; Ez 32:8; Am 5:18; Mi 7:8-9; and many others.

At this point we have compiled sufficient evidence to show that when the Bible speaks of the various ultimate ends of God's works, these ends should plainly be understood as one thing, *the glory of God*. At first view all his ends for creating the world may seem distinct, but all of them should be summarized together by this wholistic phrase. As to the best short definition of the glory of God, remember, it is God's internal glory or fullness existing in its emanating, flowing communication.

27

Conclusion: Eternally Growing Union with God

In the previous chapter, I labored to show that God's internal glory and his external glory are the same glory. There is a singularity (oneness) to the purpose God had in creating the world. Thus his internal glory and his external glory are not ultimately distinct from one another or at odds.

In this final chapter, my goal is to show how there can be consistency between God doing all things for his own glory as his ultimate end and God seeking the good of his creatures as his ultimate end. How can both of these be true at the same time and God have only one supreme end in creating the world?

> B. God's respect for himself and his good to the creature are two aspects of the same eternal glory.

As detailed earlier, when God seeks himself as his own ultimate end, he is also seeking the creature's good. Yet in seeking the creature's good, his *primary and supreme regard* in it is for himself. This is because God is both the source and the final object of the emanation of his divine glory.

God as the source and object of emanating glory

While the communication of his divine fullness (consisting of knowledge, holiness, and happiness) is related both to God and the creature, it *begins* with him. Internally, he is the fullness that is being communicated. His being is the foundation of it. The water that flows from the fountain is something of the fountain, and the beams that flow from the sun are something of the sun. God is the fountain and source of the glory that flows from him.

Not only does the emanating glory of God begin with him, it also *ends* with him. He is the object of it. After all, the knowledge that is communicated is knowledge *of God*. The love communicated is love *for God*. And the happiness communicated is joy *in God*. This means when a created being knows God, esteems him, loves him, rejoices in him, and praises him, then the glory of God is both exhibited and acknowledged. In other words, his divine fullness is both received and returned to him.

Indeed, his glory flows as both emanation and a re-emanation. It flows from God and then back to him. The radiant light of God's glory shines on and into the creature, then it is reflected back to the luminary. The beams of glory coming from God are something of God and are refunded back to their original. This means the entire enterprise of God's glory is *of* God, *in* God, and *to* God. He is the beginning, the middle, and the end.

Now, it is certainly true that when God created, he had the creature in mind with all these things. His intent was for their good. But his respect to himself and his respect to the creature are not equally divided. His respect and value for himself is much higher. It is likely that what was said in the first division of this work (Sections III and IV) is sufficient to show this. Nevertheless, it may be wise to briefly say a few more things concerning this point.

When God was about to create the world, his primary concern was the emanation of his glory. We know this because this is the actual result of his creation. In other words, it is what has actually happened and what is happening. His desire was for creation to be an arena for the emanation of radiant glory from himself, a communication of his fullness of being. Furthermore, he desired for this flowing glory to be *returned* to him as its final term. Thus he also designed his glory to flow *to the creature,* who could receive and return it.

The reason God regarded his flowing glory as a thing of great value is because he had a supreme regard and respect for himself. He placed such a high regard upon himself precisely because he placed such value on his own infinite, internal glory. It was this original value for himself that moved God to value the flowing of his glory. The infinitely high esteem he placed upon his internal glory led him to flow it outward in an external glory.

Another way to say this: God had such high regard for his glorious perfections of wisdom, righteousness, and the others, that he also valued the proper exercise of these perfections. He valued their actual working, and he valued the effect these perfections would have when they were working in the form of wise and righteous acts.

Likewise, it was because of his infinite value for his internal glory and fullness, that he also valued the *external glory* as it was communicated. He valued it for what it is in itself, not as a means to some other end (ultimately, not subordinately). He also valued his flowing glory once it entered inside the creature, since the creature experienced it in a similar way he does in terms of knowledge, holiness, and happiness.

Eternal union with God for the glory of God

Since God infinitely values his own glory, he also values the reflected image of it, which he sees in his people as his glory is communicated to them and as they participate in it. It is because he values it first within himself that he values it in them, especially since he himself is the object of their knowledge, love, and joy.

As stated much earlier in this work, it is a necessary consequence of true esteem and love that we value the esteem other people place on the same object of our affection. It also works the other way around. When a person dislikes what we dislike, we place great value on that as well. This is exactly why God heartily approves when others esteem and love him, since he himself is the object of his own love.

So taking all this together, it is easy to see how God would greatly desire and seek the good of the creature and do so from a supreme regard for himself. He longs for his creatures to gain knowledge, holiness, and even happiness, because in all these things he is glorified.

God's own happiness arises from that reflective image and participation in his own beauty. This reflection and participation happens when people behold God's glory, highly esteem and love it, and rejoice in it. It also happens when people carry out his love in the world, testifying of it to others, and displaying supreme respect for God. When a creature made by God does all these things, it is the same as saying that the creature is exalting God as his chief good and making God his supreme end.

So God, in creating the world, made *himself* his own end. This is true even though the emanation of God's fullness, which he made to flow through his creative acts, is *to* the creature. They are the object of this flowing glory. Still, God's end in creation is ultimately himself. Again, this is true even if the recipients of God's communicated fullness are incredibly benefited by that communication. Even still, God's end in creation is ultimately himself. It does not follow from the creature being benefited that God had any other end in mind than himself when he created the world.

Happiness and glory not divided goals

This leads us to the reality that the creature's true good and God's adoration of himself are both united *as one thing*. They are not divided goals. After all, the happiness that the creature aims at is a happiness that is only found when he is in union with God, and this union is what brings God glory. In fact, true happiness will rise no further than the height of union between the creature and God. A man's level of happiness and his level of union with God rise and fall together. The more true happiness he has, the greater the union he has with God. So when God makes the happiness of the creature his ultimate end, he is making his own glory his ultimate end.

All these points being true, when the creature has perfect happiness, then that means his union with God is perfect, for that is the purpose for which God made him. For all of eternity, God's creature will grow in the happiness he has in the Lord. That means the union between the creature and God will also grow more and more strict and perfect. Their relationship will always be looking more and more like the relationship between God the Father and God the Son, who are so united that their interests are perfectly one. When viewing this from the standpoint of eternity, both the happiness of the creature and the closeness of his union with God will be growing and progressing in an infinite way and in eternal duration.

Never-ending growth of happiness

Because of the duration provided by an eternal framework, the person who is in union with God must be considered as united to God in an infinite type of strictness. This is true even though there will be an ever-increasing *progress* of union with God.

It has to be so, for if God is concerned for a person that he views as having everlasting duration, then the happiness of that person and his union with God will always be rising higher and higher. This growth of joy and union will never end. Indeed, we shouldn't even think that the *rate of growth* will ever diminish. In fact, it will likely increase over the entire eternal duration.

All this being the case, God would consider the union between himself and that person, the entire whole of it, as being a complete infinite in height. He would relate to it as such. From his perspective his union with this creature would be considered perfect and complete, even though there never will be a particular time when someone can say the union has actually reached such a height, since it is an eternal progress.

To illustrate this, think of an object that stands at an infinite height above us. This represents the most perfect, complete union with God. Now, think of some object that is ascending constantly towards that infinite height. This represents the eternally increasing union of the saints with God. This object is moving upwards at a given velocity and continues to move in this way for all of eternity.

From God's point of view, he sees this entire process. He watches the object moving eternally towards the infinite height, but sees it from his unique divine angle. From his eternal perspective, he views the object as *having already* reached the infinite height. He alone has the capacity to see it as complete. And if he personally relates to this complete and perfect union (as he sees it) as the end he had in mind for creation, and makes it his ultimate end, then he certainly respects it as an infinite height. This is true though the time will never come when one of the saints can say he has *actually arrived* at this infinite height.

The motions of the created order

Here is another way to say this: The ultimate end God aims at is the very thing which the motions he causes aims at. If he begins a progression that is moving and tending towards a certain goal, then that goal is what he is ultimately aiming at.

To illustrate, suppose a number of objects have been made. By appointment, these objects make a constant, eternal movement towards a certain center. This being the case, it appears that the person who made these objects and caused their motion was *aiming at the center*. After all, this is where their motion is pointing. This is the direction they are eternally going. From their motion we can determine that the center is what they are eternally striving after.

If God himself is this center, then God aimed at himself as his own ultimate end when he created the world. If God is the Author of the being and motion of all the things he has made, then he is also their Last End. He is their final term, the center to which they tend, and where they are ultimately aimed.

Thus we can judge what end the Creator had in mind when he created the world by observing the things he made. When we see the types of things he made, what kinds of beings they are, and what they lean and progress towards for eternity, then the Creator's ultimate end should become visible to our understanding. This is true even though the time will never come when it can be said to have attained in the most absolute perfect manner from our perspective.

Though this attainment will never happen *from our perspective*, we must understand that the interest of the creature should be considered one with the interest of God. This is because the strictness of union with God is viewed as infinitely complete *from his perspective*. Even though it is an ever-increasing type of progress, nonetheless, the interests of God and his people should be properly thought of as undivided. They are not separate or disjoined from his eternal perspective.

There might still be difficulties in understanding how God might do this. Some might wonder how to reconcile the fact that God did not make the creature his ultimate end (in some way separate from making himself his ultimate end), with God's benevolence and free grace and with the creature's obligation to gratitude. This objection was answered thoroughly in the first division of this work (Section IV, Objection 4). The point I'm making for our purposes here pertains to the ultimate unity of the creature and God, uniting their interests together as one.

Happiness and glory: the same pursuit

To illustrate this point, consider a man and his family who have a strict union with each other. It may be said that their interests are one. If this is so, how much more are the interests of Christ and his church united as one? They are united in an unspeakable more perfect and exalted way. In heaven this union of interests between Christ and his church will be infinitely closer than it ever could be between an earthy father and his family.

We also do well to remember that the union of Christ and his church is eternal and thus ever-increasing. Earthly families are simply unable to enjoy this type of union.

We are also justified in seeing the interests of God and his people as so united that they can be sought in an undivided manner, not as distinct, separate pursuits. *To pursue one is to pursue the other.* In pursing the interests of his people, who stand in eternal union with him, God pursues his own interests. And in pursuing the interests of God, his people are pursuing their own interests, for when he is glorified, they are benefited by it.

This is what God aimed at when he created the world, and it can be summarized by that one overarching phrase, *the glory of God.* This is God's ultimate end for creating the world. It is the good thing he designed all of creation to produce. And it must be understood from his point of view, since he sees the entire duration of it as one whole thing, his people in eternal union with him.

Someone might raise an objection here, but it is not a solid one. It might be said that God could not have been aiming at the infinitely perfect union between himself and his people, since the union between them will never be infinitely perfect and complete. After all, it is the type of thing that increases forever without end.

But a comparison to eternal damnation will show this objection to be weak. God aims at satisfying his infinite justice through the eternal damnation of sinners. Their damnation will satisfy eternal justice precisely because of its eternal duration. If their punishment was not eternal, it could not completely satisfy God's justice, nor could anything else. However, there will never be a time when someone can say, "Now, justice is satisfied."

Of course, our modern free-thinkers will not accept this. They do not like talking about satisfying justice with infinite punishment.

But nobody denies that God aims to satisfy his grace and benevolence in heaven. He does this by glorifying the saints there with eternal blessing. He bestows upon them that which is good and infinitely valuable, precisely because it is *eternal in duration*. However, there will never come a moment when an individual can say (from his limited perspective), "Now this infinitely valuable good has actually and completely been bestowed," since there will never be an end to it.

Conclusion of the Work

This brings the work to a final conclusion. I hope that it has been made clear from both the realm of reason and the sacred Scriptures that God aimed at his own glory as his ultimate end when he created the world. This ultimate end is not inconsistent in any way with God's desire to bring knowledge, holiness, and happiness to the creatures he created. They are, for all practical purposes, the same pursuit. Therefore, may God be glorified!

OUTLINE

The following outline is designed to provide readers with a bird's eye view of *The End for Which God Created the World*. A couple of items should be noted.

First, I did take the liberty to add clarifying sub-points where I believed they helped illuminate Edwards' points. A comparison with Edwards' original texts will show the few places I took this liberty.

Secondly, the chapter divisions are mine, not Edwards'. These were added to break the text up into basically equal, bite-sized sections and to give broad topical headings to guide the reader. They are included in the outline (bold left) as a reference point.

1: Chief Ends and Ultimate Ends
    Introduction
        I. Explanation of terms and general positions
            A. Understanding subordinate ends
            B. Understanding ultimate ends
            C. Relationships between subordinate and ultimate ends
            D. Understanding chief ends

2: More about Ends and How They Work
        II. Expanded explanation of terms and general positions
            A. Subordinate ends can never be more valuable than the ultimate end(s) to which they are subordinate.
            B. The ultimate end is always superior in value to any of the subordinate ends connected to it.
            C. A being has a supreme end if he has only one end in mind for everything he does.
            D. An ultimate end is one that is loved for its own sake.

3: God and Ultimate Ends

E. Seeking a singular thing means there can be only one ultimate end.

F. The original ultimate end alone is what motivated God to create the world.

G. God's ultimate end in creating the world must be the same ultimate end he has for all his works.

H. God's ultimate end in his works of providence in general is the same as his ultimate end for creation.

I. There can be only one supreme last end of God's work.

4: Division One: Help from Reason

SECTION I: Some general observations from reason about why God created the world

A. God is not in any way dependent upon what he has made, nor did he create the world as a result of some personal insufficiency.

B. The existence of God precedes any actions he performs, which means his existence cannot be the ultimate goal of any of his actions.

C. God's ultimate end in creating the world must have the following three attributes: It must be original or prior to the creation of the world, it must be the most valuable thing in itself, and it must be something capable of being attained by his act of creation.

5: God's Obligation to Be His Own Ultimate End

D. If it is possible for God to be his own ultimate end in creating the world, then he is morally obligated to do so.

E. Whatever God aimed at in the creation of the world (that is good and valuable in itself) must be what God aims at ultimately.

F. When an effect or consequence is caused by the creation of the world (that is simply and absolutely good and valuable in itself) that thing is an ultimate end in God's creating the world.

6: The Flowing Glory of God
  SECTION II: Some further observations from reason about why God created the world
    A. The exertion of God's glorious attributes is something that seems fit, proper, and desirable in itself.
    B. It also seems fit, proper, and desirable in itself that the glorious perfections of God should be known by other persons besides himself.
    C. Other beings should love and delight in seeing and knowing the glory of God.
    D. The full goodness of God should flow forth as streams from an infinite fountain of good.

7: God's Supreme Respect for Himself
  SECTION III: A list of how God shows a supreme and ultimate respect for himself in all his works
    A. God shows supreme respect for himself through the operations and exertions of his perfect attributes.
    B. God shows supreme respect for himself by loving when others know him, delight in him, and love him.
    C. God shows supreme respect for himself when his full goodness flows forth like an infinite fountain.

8: God Is Glorified in the Communications of Himself
    - Glory to God when he communicates his knowledge to the creature
    - Glory to God when he communicates his holiness to the creature
    - Glory to God when he communicates his happiness to the creature

9: The Objection of Inconsistency
  SECTION IV: Some objections considered against the reasonable nature of the arguments made
    Objection 1: God seeking himself would be inconsistent with his own character.
      Answer 1: Wrong notions of God's happiness

>   Answer 2: No better alternative
>   Answer 3: God's self-sufficiency actually diminished by the opposite view

10: The Objection of Selfishness
> *Objection 2:* God would be selfish if he were his own last end.
>> Answer 1: Careless notions of selfishness and generosity
>> Answer 2: Benefit for the general public
>> Answer 3: God's good and the good of his creatures

11: The Objection of Unworthiness
> *Objection 3:* It would be unworthy of God to seek delight from his creatures.
>> Answer 1: Valuing the most valuable thing
>> Answer 2: Grace leads to honor
>> Answer 3: The value of wise and just esteem

12: The Objection of Freeness and Obligation
> *Objection 4:* Divine freeness and creaturely obligation would be in jeopardy if God were his own last end.
>> Answer 1: Not at odds
>> Answer 2: Possible inconsistencies not applicable to God

13: Second Division: What Scripture Teaches
> **SECTION I:** Basic overview
> **SECTION II:** Some interpretive positions
>> *Position 1:* God's ultimate end for his works of providence in general is the same as his ultimate end for all of creation.
>> *Position 2:* God's ultimate end can be discerned from passages that mention only some of God's works of providence.
>> *Position 3:* God's ultimate end can be discerned from frequent mention.
>> *Position 4:* God's ultimate end for the moral system is the same as his ultimate end for all of creation.

Position 5: God's ultimate end for his most significant works of providence is the same as his ultimate end for all of creation.

Position 6: God's ultimate end for his most significant works of providence in the moral world is the same as his ultimate end for all of creation.

Position 7: God's ultimate end in the part of the moral world that is good is the same as his ultimate end for all of creation.

Position 8: God's ultimate end for the moral code of conduct given to his moral agents is the same as his ultimate end for all of creation.

Position 9: God's ultimate end for the goodness in the good part of the moral world is the same as his ultimate end for all of creation.

Position 10: God's ultimate end for his approved saints is the same as his ultimate end for all of creation.

Position 11: God's ultimate end for holy living is the same as his ultimate end for all of creation.

Position 12: The ultimate end sought by Jesus Christ is the same as God's ultimate end for all of creation.

14: Scriptural Demonstrations of God's Glory as His Ultimate End

SECTION III: Scriptural demonstrations of God's Glory as his ultimate end in creating the world

Demonstration 1: Passages that present God's glory as the ultimate end of all his works

Demonstration 2: Passages that present God's glory as the ultimate end of the good part of the moral world

15: Demonstrations Concerning the Moral Part of Creation

Demonstration 3: Passages that present God's glory as the ultimate end for the goodness of the moral part of creation

Demonstration 4: Passages that present God's requirement that people do everything to glorify him

Demonstration 5: Passages that present God's glory as the ultimate end for what delights the best part of the moral world

16: Redemption in Jesus for the Glory of God
>*Demonstration 6:* Passages that present God's glory as the ultimate end sought by Jesus Christ
>
>*Demonstration 7:* Passages that present redemption as being for the glory of God

17: The Ultimate End of Judgment Day and All Works of Providence
>*Demonstration 8:* Passages that present all moral goodness as being for the glory of God
>
>*Demonstration 9:* Passages that present God's general works of providence as being for his glory

18: For the Sake of His Name
>**SECTION IV:** For the sake of his name, so that his perfections will be known, and so that he will be praised
>
>A. For the sake of his name

19: An Arena for His Perfections to Be Known
>B. To make his perfections known

20: For the Praise of his Glory
>C. So that he will be praised

21: The Good of the Creature and the Glory of God
>**SECTION V:** The communication of good to his creatures as an ultimate end
>>A. The communication of good is an ultimate end.
>>
>>B. Redemption through Jesus is not a mere subordinate end.
>>
>>C. God communicates good to his creatures for the sake of his own goodness and mercy.
>>
>>D. God's governing acts communicate his goodness.

22: The Happiness of God's People
>>E. God uses all creation for the good of his people.
>>
>>F. God judges the wicked for the good of his people.
>>
>>G. God pours out his eternal goodness.
>>
>>H. All of God's works are for goodness and mercy.

  I. God's works of providence are for the good of his people.
  J. The deeds of God's people fulfill his ultimate purpose.

23: Scripture on the Internal Glory of God
  SECTION VI: A consideration of the biblical phrases "glory of God" and "name of God"
    A. Scriptural analysis of the phrase "glory of God"
      1: Internal glory

24: Scripture on the Communicated Glory of God
      2: Communicated glory

25: Scripture on the Viewing and Praising of God's Glory
      3: Received and viewed glory
      4: Praised glory
    B. Scriptural analysis of the phrase "name of God"

26: The Oneness of God's Ultimate End
  SECTION VII: Only one ultimate end and what it is
    A. God's internal glory and external glory are the same glory.

27: Eternal, Ever-growing Union with God
    B. God's respect for himself and his good to the creature are two aspects of the same eternal glory.
  Conclusion of the Work

Acknowledgments

This book would not have been possible without the power and love of the Lord. He deserves all the credit for any good that comes from it. I thank him for providing me the opportunity to bring this project to completion, and I honor him for allowing me to worship his glory while I worked.

I also express my deep appreciation to Jonathan Edwards. He currently resides in the great cloud of witnesses (Hebrews 12:1), and I'm hopeful to have conversations with him one day, though I'm sure the line will be long. Obviously, his impact on my own heart has been tremendous, and I pray that he will speak on to a world that truly needs to hear his voice.

Thank you to Dr. John Piper who first planted a love in my heart for Edwards' writings. I am amazed at how much these two men are alike and how God used them both to greatly influence their respective generations.

I would also like to mention Kelly Bridges who diligently proofread the entire manuscript, finding multiple mistakes. She improved the text and offered many suggestions and encouragements. I am grateful for her labor.

Many thanks also to my precious wife, Page, and our five children. My heart overflows with gratitude for my sweet and supportive family.

Finally, I want to thank the congregation at Rock Mountain Lakes Baptist Church for allowing me to be your pastor. You are so supportive and loving, and I can't express in words how much satisfaction I receive serving the Lord with you. I pray that the same depth of passion and zeal that Jonathan Edwards exhibited in worship would be cultivated within every member of our flock. God is truly worthy of our deepest adoration and praise!

Printed in Great Britain
by Amazon.co.uk, Ltd.,
Marston Gate.